BORN

TO

DREAM

BORN

— TO —

DREAM

ROLLAN A. ROBERTS II

Kat Ranch
PUBLISHING

Published by Kat Ranch Publishing
140 South Main Street | Brooksville, FL 34601 USA

Book design copyright © 2009 by Tate Publishing, LLC. All rights reserved.
Cover design by Lance Waldrop
Interior design by Stefanie Rooney

Published in the United States of America

ISBN: 978-0-9823798-1-3
1. Self Help, Dreams 2. Self Help, Personal Growth, Success

This book is dedicated to every dreamer that has the courage to keep their vision alive and keep on believing that their dreams will manifest themselves in a tangible way. I know they are already your reality!

TABLE OF CONTENTS

FOREWORD

There are many books that speak about purpose and success, but none of them come close to tapping into the heart like *Born to Dream*. Rollan truly rose to his calling of "Dream Builder" in this amazing work. If you aren't sure what your purpose on earth is yet, *Born to Dream* will give you the questions to ask to find it. If you have unfulfilled goals and dreams, keep reading; Rollan breaks down exactly what you must do to fulfill your maximum potential.

This is not just another goal-setting book filled with motivational hype. This concise, thought-provoking book will change the way you view your goals and dreams forever. The premise of the book—that dreams are not things—not only revolutionizes how to achieve unprecedented success, but also turns the traditional thinking in the personal development industry upside down.

Every chapter is packed with powerful ideas and techniques to realize tangible results. Regardless of how insignificant your dreams may seem or how big your dreams may be, you will be armed with the ammunition you need to take action and conquer everything that would try to deter you. Following the unique format of his first book, *Born to be Rich*, you will once again be left with "Reflections on the Riches from this Chapter" that highlight the primary elements to focus on.

You won't find hoopla or theory in the next few pages, but you will find the keys required to living a happy and blessed life. I have been inspired by Rollan and his devotion and commitment to helping people around the world live their dreams. Your destiny awaits you in *Born to Dream.*

CAROL CARLAN

CEO, Carlan Consulting
Past West Panhandle President, Wachovia Bank

INTRODUCTION

When I was a kid, people would always ask me what I wanted to be when I grew up. Interestingly enough, they never asked me what I wanted to *do*. Somewhere along the line, and it usually is around the time bills start rolling in, the question becomes much less about what you want to *be* and much more about what you must *do*. Many of us wanted to be firemen, policemen, cowboys, princesses, royalty, heroes, artists, musicians, writers, farmers, professional athletes, or movie stars.

Granted, the reason many of us are not some of the things we have wanted to be in the past is because our priorities have changed and grown, and we've become different people. We want to be and do different things now. I remember as a middle school student wanting to work at Taco Bell when I grew up. I thought they had the coolest job ever! They could have soft tacos and Nacho Supremes whenever they wanted. I mean, how much better can life get?

Thanks to Roy Rogers, John Wayne, and other classic Western cowboys, I wanted to be a cowboy on a ranch out west more than anything else. In fact, I spent two summers working as a ranch hand in Tennessee with three other cowboys tending 110 horses. We gave two forty-five-minute trail rides and one ninety-minute trail ride each day with morning and evening steak cookouts. I went from that dream to wanting to be a Navy Seal, CIA operative, or SWAT team member. I worked out tediously and methodically so I would be ready physically.

Take a moment and think back on all the things you

wanted to be as you were growing up. Now, I want you to stop reading for just a second.

Here you are, right here, right now, and just like in your childhood, teenage years, college days, and up to this moment, you have an idea in your mind of who and what you want to be. You know what you want your body to look like. You have a picture of what kind of lifestyle you want to have. You have a mental image of how your family should operate. You imagine the cars that you want to have. You know what color the exterior is; you know what color the interior is; you know what the leather smells like; you know how fast it goes; you know how much it costs. You know the schools you want your children to attend. You know the faith you want to instill in your kids. You know the vacations you want to take. You know the friends you want to have and that you want your children to have. What I'm saying is you now have, at this moment, a mental picture of what you want out of life just like you did when you were a child. The difference between now and times past is that you have the conscious will, sound mind, and decision-making ability to set those dreams in stone.

You can decide right now that you won't settle for less. Oh, you will always be thankful for what you have, but you will never stop pursuing the dream that lies within you. You can decide right now that you will not settle for good, knowing you were destined for greatness. You can decide right now that this life is too short to waste on little dreams and small goals. You will pursue; you will engage; you will confront; you will move on; you will keep going; you will not quit; you will not stop; you will not give up until you have achieved the dream that lies within you. This book is for those of you that used to dream, but life has beaten you up. Life told you that the good life is only for certain people. Life told you that it takes luck to achieve the greatness you're looking for, and you've decided you're not a lucky person. This book is for you. This book is for the person that is stale, stagnant, and thinks what they have and what they've achieved is all they will get or do. It's for those who are done living. It's for those who think life's not worth living anymore. It's for those who have a dream but are questioning whether or not the dream is worth living for. It's for those who are questioning the price they are paying to achieve their dreams.

I'm so glad this book is also for those of you who have a burning passion within you bright enough and hot enough to light up the night sky ten times over. You are so committed to reaching your goals and dreams that you could run right through ten tractor trailers going ninety miles per hour and a herd of raging bulls. You're willing to cross deserts, swim oceans, and climb mountains to reach your dreams. You're willing to do the impossible. You're willing to give life all you've got without counting the cost or playing it safe. You're chasing your dreams with a fury. People may not know where you're going, but they know you're going somewhere. This book is for you, my friend. You think you're fired up now? Just wait! You won't even be able to make it through this book in one sitting because you will get so excited, you'll have to put the book down to go take action! That's what this book will do for you.

This book will fan the flame if you are already in hot pursuit of your dreams. This book will reignite the dreams you used to believe in. This book will help you define your dream if you've never looked at life this way before. Regardless of where you are in life now, you will walk away from *Born to Dream* a new person. You will wear a different smile. You will have a different beat to your step. Your life does have a purpose. There is a master plan for your life. Now let's find out what that plan is, do it, and live the life we were created to live!

Chapter 1

POINT A TO POINT B

So what's in a dream? Why is it worth reading book after book about finding, defining, and pursuing a dream? What would life be like if we did not dream, if we had no goals to shoot for and no hope of a better life? What if we were not built with any ambition? What if the pure desire to be more, do more, and achieve more was never instilled in us?

This is a worthy thought because our dreams are either worth every ounce of energy, finances, and persistence we have, or they aren't. Either they are something to be suppressed or they are visions—a type of instruction—of what we are to make of our lives.

Dreams move us through the various stages of our lives. We spend our academic years dreaming of graduation. The dream of graduating keeps young people all over the world up late studying, working on homework, working hard, completing projects, learning foreign languages, the sciences, and the arts—for thirteen years! It is a dream and accomplishment that is significant. In fact, so many people have achieved that dream that entire businesses have grown out of that general accomplishment. So having a dream and worthwhile goal took most of us through the first part of our lives.

Upon graduating from high school, every young person is

forced to make a decision. They can go to college. They can get a job. They can stay at home with mom and dad and do nothing. They can volunteer. They can start a business. There are a number of choices a young person that just graduated from high school can make. What will guide their decision? Parents can be quite influential in making this decision. Friends certainly play a role. Perhaps a mentor, teacher, or coach has had a significant impact. Ultimately, it comes down to the young person's decision. They may weigh the feedback and advice that each one of these influential parties has given, but in the end, it is their call. What makes a young person choose one path or opportunity over another? It is their dream. Now they may not be consciously thinking about this, which is scary enough, but their decision usually comes down to what they feel is the right thing for them in their lives, or it is something they strongly desire.

As strange as it seems in our culture today, their decision is neither right nor wrong. There are certainly specific repercussions and consequences for each path, such as not pursuing their education, but the most important thing is to pursue the dream that is inside you. If you choose to go to college, then the dream of graduating with a degree spurs you to push yourself emotionally, physically, financially, and come test time, spiritually. Upon graduation, the typical person at that point gets a job and starts their career. After a short period of time in the work place, the young person decides that their ideas and management style are more preferable than that of their boss, so they determine to pursue a promotion. After a couple or three years, they seek the next level. Most companies only promote an employee two or three times at the most, so when another couple years go by, and they start seeking another promotion, they switch jobs and keep moving up. Call it ambition; call it overachieving; call it what you will, but it is the dream that keeps people pushing forward. The dream is that element within you that makes you get excited and fired up. You couldn't sit still if you wanted to because you feel so overwhelmed. I feel that way when I look at luxury home magazines, amazing yachts, private jets, and resort vacations. It's not because those things are my dream. I just know that when I've achieved my dreams, I will have those things as well. Those things are a way for me to tell how close I am to achieving my dream.

If you and I were standing on the top of a skyscraper and the next skyscraper was fifty feet away, would you cross a foot-wide plank between the two for free? What if I told you I'd give you $100? Would you do it for $1000? How about a million? Maybe there's a dollar amount that you would go for and maybe not. But let's say that you have a child that you love more than anything else in this world. They mean more to you than life itself. Let's imagine that your child is being abducted from the top of the other skyscraper. I don't know a parent in this world that wouldn't risk life and limb, lay aside all inhibitions, logic, reason, and common sense, and dart across the plank in attempt to save their child's life. That's because the dream is big enough that all of the obstacles don't really matter. What they wouldn't do for money, fame, and fortune, they would do for a dream that consumed them.

That's the kind of dream this book is about. This isn't about the casual daydreamer who is just hoping to achieve something. I'm talking about the kind of dream where it is already your reality; you're just waiting for it to become tangible so everyone else knows it is your reality! The reason most people don't have the material wealth they are seeking in this life is because they don't have a dream that is big enough to reach it.

The goal doesn't have to be more money, faster cars, or fancier homes. The dream may be to grow your business to certain revenue levels. Your dream may be to invest specific amounts of money. Your dream may be to reduce poverty, empower underprivileged children, or teach financial literacy to the masses. Regardless, you can achieve your dreams. If your dream does not give you the lifestyle you are looking for, then it is likely that your dream is not big enough. A by-product of accomplishing your dream is the acquisition of the things and lifestyle you want in this life. This is why it is critical that your life's purpose and dream be aligned.

I've met several people through the years that did not want to dream. They told me they didn't want to get their hopes up and get all excited about something again if it wasn't going to happen. I truly understand how these people feel, but I also understand that if the dream is big enough, you will find a way to make it happen. You will find the opportunity that will bring about the desires of your heart. There are many possibilities that may have kept you from realizing your dream. Most people make the mistake of chasing a pension instead of their passion. They are too busy chasing money when they should be chasing their dream!

I don't chase the car. The car is just a reward when I achieve my dream. I don't chase the jet, the yacht, the mansion, or the vacations. They are the by-products of the accomplishment of my dreams. I guess my challenge in understanding the "I don't want to dream because I don't want to be let down again" mentality is that I can't turn my dream off and on. It's either there or it's not. If it's not, this book will give you some questions you can ask yourself to define your dream and your purpose.

There is no stopping point in my dream. There is not a halftime where I can say, "It's over. I'm not going to win." I want to inspire others to pursue their dreams, get their eyes off the obstacles, and focus on the prize before them. Nowhere in that dream have I helped enough people. I must help the next person and the next person and the next. So go ahead. Get excited! Get fired up! Let your imagination carry you to places you have not dared to dream before. Don't hold back. The second you think you're going overboard and dreaming too big, you need to stop right there and clearly define that picture because it is very likely that is where you're supposed to be. Let yourself dream what your life will be like as you see success from the realization of your dream.

So why dream? Because you already do and use it to your benefit, just not on the scale that is available to you! Every accomplishment, accolade, promotion, and emotionally gratifying experience you have ever had was the realization of a dream. I want you to dream on purpose. I don't want it to happen by accident because you will never be, or do, or have all that you can be, do, and have if you refuse to recognize and implement the power that comes from having a dream, defining a dream, chasing a dream, and keeping the dream alive.

Reflections on the Riches from This Chapter

☞ Decide right now that you will not settle for good, knowing you were destined for greatness.

☞ You will pursue; you will engage; you will confront; you will move on; you will keep going; you will not quit; you will not stop; you will not give up until you have achieved the dream that lies within you.

☞ What you won't do for money, fame, and fortune, you will do for a dream that consumes you.

☞ Most people are too busy chasing money instead of their dreams!

Chapter 2

IT'S JUST THE BEGINNING

M ost people today don't even realize what sparks their ambition or drives them to pursue success the way they do. It's the power of a dream! I want you to look past money now. Many people confuse dreams with money or things. That is because money and things have become symbols of glory and success. Dreams aren't merely a wish list, just as everything you want is not your dream. A dream is not what you want to have but who you want to be. It's about personal accomplishment and success. People can set anything as a goal or dream, but the most worthwhile dreams involve the purpose for which you are here. The most powerful, most fulfilling dream you can possibly have is one that allows you to do what you are passionate about and love to do every day while having the life and lifestyle that you desire.

Desires are very interesting to observe. I remember a particular house in the neighborhood I grew up in. I thought the people who lived there were super rich. I just knew that if I ever had a million dollars, that's where I'd live. I even thought that up through high school! After I went to college, bought a house, and started investing in real estate, I changed my mind about spending my future fortune on one of the houses in the neighborhood I grew up in.

I decided that really rich people live on lakes. So I worked, invested, and bought a lake house. After I had lived in the lake house for a period of time, I discovered that rich people don't just have one house, they have two. Then I heard about rich people who had a ranch out west with hundreds or thousands of acres with horses roaming on the property, beautiful barns, stately fences, and a massive main house with multiple guest houses.

Just when I thought there couldn't be more than that, you discover those same rich people need their own private getaway on the coast. But their beach front home isn't like the ones I had been in. Their beach front homes are estates in and of themselves. They are ten thousand plus square feet with dual winding staircases, marble everywhere, and vast expansive ocean views. They also need a summer home in the Hamptons and a chateau in Italy. New Zealand and Venice are beckoning them to buy.

The point is that at each stage in my life, I thought that was as good as it gets. I thought that was the peak and pinnacle of success. I went through the same evolution with cars. You could have given me a million dollars when I was seventeen, and I would have bought a convertible Ford Mustang and a Ford Thunderbird! You and I, regardless of where we are at this point in our lives, don't know what we don't know. I still don't know what I don't know.

I think this is one of the most wonderful parts of being a dreamer. Dreams don't stand still. They don't stagnate. The more you dream, the bigger they get. I see this demonstrated in all types of sports. A basketball player has a dream of scoring twenty points in a game. He finally scores twenty points for the first time in a game. He can't believe it, but the next thing you know, twenty is the new standard. He doesn't have a good game unless he scores twenty. However, he would have to score twenty-five points to have a great game. Once he hits twenty-five, thirty becomes the new dream.

Dreams grow. The more you dream, the more you achieve. The more you achieve, the bigger your dream gets. Your desire for continued excellence continues to grow with each victory and accomplishment. I don't know how great I can be because I'm not at the end yet. You don't know how great you can be because you're still breathing. You can keep growing, keep dreaming, and keep doing the impossible. Look, we don't know where the line is to greatness. Our responsibility is to keep improving upon the success that we have had or that has been set by others.

Individual greatness means many things to so many people. I hear people refer to others as "a great employee" or "a great teacher." You hear people talking about great athletes, great leaders, and great thinkers. Greatness oftentimes refers to a person's very essence, and other times it is used to describe the incredible talent and skills that one has developed.

Every human being has the potential for greatness. There is no circumstance too dire, no odds too insurmountable, and no dream too great that one human being with an insatiable, relentless determination cannot overcome. Greatness must be earned. It cannot be bought. That's how you can separate the winners from the losers with the second-generation kids who inherited hundreds of millions of dollars.

True greatness is not driven by money. True greatness is not driven by houses, cars, vacations, luxury yachts, private planes, fancy clothes, and expensive jewelry. Greatness is directly tied to the human will, heart, soul, and spirit, and things can't satisfy that part of a winner. All the money and wealth this world has to offer can't console the person within whom greatness lies but has not yet blossomed. The wealth would still leave you feeling empty. That's why some people who have everything you think they want start another business, sing another song, make another album, write another book, buy another investment property, play another game, and keep on doing what they do best. It's because of greatness.

Big dreams demand greatness. Dreams should be in sight, but out of reach. Your dreams should demand that the greatness inside of you rise up and manifest itself to help you become the person you were meant to be. Only then can you realize the dreams you were destined to dream and live and breathe the air you were destined to live and breathe. The sun will be brighter; people will be friendlier, and the sky will be bluer. We don't know how great life can get or just how good we can be. It's up to you and me to keep dreaming so we can know then what we don't know now.

Reflections on the Riches from This Chapter

☞ Dreams aren't merely a wish list, just as everything you want is not your dream.

☞ A dream is not what you want to have but who you want to be.

☞ Our responsibility is to keep improving upon the success that we have had or that has been set by others.

☞ All the money and wealth this world has to offer can't console the person within whom greatness lies but has not yet blossomed.

☞ Dreams should be in sight and out of reach.

Chapter 3

LIFESTYLE ARCHITECTURE

W hen I ask most people what their dream is, I usually hear things like freedom, time, houses, sports cars, luxury cars, and the like. Parents want to be free from their job so they can spend time with the family doing what they want to do. They want to work for themselves instead of someone else. They want to be in control of their own schedules and not have to coordinate their vacation around the schedules of others. They don't want to rely on a boss to tell them how much money they are going to make next year, which, in turn, tells them what kind of house they can live in, cars they can drive, and vacations they can take. These are certainly worthwhile lifestyle goals to have. However, that is not the essence of your dream. I'm going to give you ten questions you can ask yourself to define your dream.

1. What are you really passionate about in life?

No doubt, you are probably good at a lot of things. I'm good at a lot of things. That doesn't mean I want to do all of the things I'm good at. So what are the one or two things you do that make you feel most alive when you do them? What activities are you engaged in when you feel most successful?

I feel this way every time I speak to a group of people. I

absolutely love and thrive on inspiring other people and challenging them to pursue their dreams and giving them tools to help them do so. There is no greater feeling in the world to me. I love being fired up. I love the moment when an audience and I connect. I always walk out wishing it didn't have to end and looking forward to the next time I get to speak.

I am passionate about your success. I am more concerned about your success than I am about mine. I am called to help those who want to be helped, inspire those who want to be inspired, and challenge those who need to be challenged. I feel most successful when I finish a meeting where I was helping, inspiring, or challenging one or more people. What in your life gives you the most enjoyment? When do you feel most fulfilled as a person? When I'm in that moment, I can't tell you how much money I have, what I own, what I drive, or where I live. None of those things really matter at that moment. The only thing that matters is the pure fulfillment of my mission and purpose from which my dream is born.

2. What bothers you?

I've heard Mike Murdock say, "What bothers you most is an indication of the problem you were created to solve." If you can define what causes you pain, it very well may be the problem you were created to solve. Murdock puts it this way: "Doctors solve medical problems; attorneys solve legal problems; garbage collectors solve refuse problems."

So what problem were you created to solve? What do you find impossible to tolerate? I cannot stand poverty. I don't like the look of it. I can't stand what it does to the human mind and the human spirit. Poverty and lack is absolutely despicable, detestable, and grotesque in its very nature. It is a disease. It eats you up from the inside out. Instead of sitting around and talking about how much I hate poverty, I declared war on it and decided to take action.

I realized early on that I can't help someone who doesn't want to be helped. It has to be their decision, not mine. So instead of trying to help everyone who would listen, which I spent several years doing, I turned to the power of the spoken and written word to fight the poverty epidemic. That way, only those who are actively seeking to better themselves and their futures come to me for mentorship. It allows me to fulfill my purpose, thus fulfilling my dream. My dream is to fulfill my purpose all the days of my life. On that journey, the dream gets bigger and bigger with the desire to help more people.

3. *What would you do or be if time and money were no object?*

It's hard for many people to think on this level because it is the only life they have ever known. What do you love doing so much that you'd do it for free if you knew all your needs were met with the lifestyle you desired? How would you invest your time?

Discovering the thing in your life that you are so passionate about that you cannot put a price tag on it will help you define your purpose. You will realize that your dream is not a thing but is actually the fulfillment and full embodiment of your purpose. Then, and only then, are you living life to the maximum. It is in that moment that you feel most alive. So what would you do and who would you be if you had all the time in the world and could instantly be whoever you wanted to be?

4. *What is your purpose in life?*

The answer to this question will give you insight into your destiny, which you must define before you can truly know what your dream is. Have you discovered why you were put on this earth? Do you see the providential hand of the Almighty placing you in the family that he wanted you to have and having the childhood that you did? Everything you need to become and all you are meant to become exists in your life right now. It is your responsibility and duty to explore and dig until you determine what is the core purpose of your existence.

I've learned that you find in life what you're looking for. If you're looking for the reasons you should buy something, you will find them. If you are looking for reasons you should not do something, you will find them. If you are looking for reasons for something or against something, you will generally find those as well. In fact, depending on what people are looking for, two people can see the exact same thing and describe it in different ways. It is because the filtering system they use to process information is programmed differently. Everything we see with our eyes is passed through a filtering process that is made up of our past experiences, education, childhood, relationships, and everything we have been through up to that point. Make it a priority to look for your purpose. Seek and ye shall find.

5. What are your natural abilities?

Everyone has been gifted with natural talents and abilities. There is something unique about you that is not common in mankind. It may be your ability to love, care, inspire, teach, or think. You may have uncommon athletic ability in a particular sport. You may be musically inclined. You may have a good sense for buying real estate, picking stocks, or putting business deals together. You may be one of the most effective people in the world in a support role. You may have exceptional organizational skills. You may be able to communicate amazingly well. You may have great charisma that immediately draws people to you. Perhaps you are mechanically inclined. Think about the simple things in life that you seem to have a natural inclination toward. Perhaps it's something that you rarely think about because it does come so naturally for you.

You have been gifted with certain inclinations, bents, and tendencies that require you to work, hone, and refine them so that you can accomplish your purpose. One way to help discover your purpose is to take stock and inventory of your natural talents and analyze how they may be used in a meaningful manner.

6. What are you complimented on most often?

The answer to this question will help you assess your natural abilities. People oftentimes don't recognize the seeds of greatness within themselves because it does come naturally. You might be great at scrapbooking or event planning and are constantly being praised for the fruits of your labor. You may be complimented on your looks, your hair, your smile, your skin, or your sense of style. You may be praised for your faithfulness, self-discipline, attention to detail, dependability, integrity, promptness, or ability to execute. The next time someone compliments you, ask yourself how you can use that talent or ability and assess what role that skill can play in the fulfillment of your purpose.

7. What would you do if you knew you only had one week to live?

This is definitely a loaded question, but it does immediately boil away everything that doesn't really matter in life. However you answer that question is a good indication of how you should spend the rest of your life, regardless of how much time is left. If there's a message you want the world to hear if you only had a week left to live, then you should start sharing that message now. If you would immediately want to be the best person, the kindest person, and the most loving person if you only had a week left to live, then you should be the best, kindest, most loving person today. What knowledge would you want to impart to your children and family? What would you tell your friends? How would you invest your time in the last few days?

I'm not advocating with this question that you spend all of your money today because who knows where we will be a week from now. I believe you should live for today and plan for tomorrow. You might find that your answers to these questions form the very essence of whom you are suppose to be and the basis of your life's work.

8. When do you feel the most successful and alive?

There are specific actions and moments in time where I have felt immensely successful. It is during those times that I felt more alive than ever before. These times were characterized by my best and highest personal performance. Think back to the times in your life when you felt immensely successful. What were you doing and what must you do to replicate that feeling of success? What do you do or say that makes you feel special, needed, or appreciated? What are you doing when you feel like you're "on" or "in the zone?"

This question, more than any other single question, helped me discover my purpose in life. I realized that I never felt more alive than when I was inspiring individuals and families in their living rooms night after night and groups of people at hotel convention centers to pursue their dreams, break through the barriers, and never give up. I felt more successful doing that than lying beachside on an island! I merely enjoy lying beachside with beachfront service, but that's not when I feel most successful. I don't feel as successful relaxing in a beautiful house or driving fancy cars as I do when I'm on the platform making a difference in the lives of the listeners. Think back to moments when you felt that same feeling of aliveness and ask yourself how that action relates to your dream and purpose.

9. What circumstances in life are unique to you, and how can you use those to your benefit?

Everyone has a story. No two people have the exact same story. The human life is a tale of tragedies and triumphs. Everyone has ups and downs. Some of the common challenging circumstances are related to finances, health, and relationships. Sometimes people lose loved ones, battle through disease, accomplish amazing victories, do the seemingly impossible, or demonstrate uncommon determination and courage in the face of adversity. What have you gone through in your life and what are some things you have learned that you can put to good use? It might not be one isolated event that took place, but you will realize the more you reflect that the combined lessons learned from each circumstance form a powerful clue into your purpose. What have the circumstances of your life been grooming you for?

10. What do you want your legacy to be?

Another way to determine your purpose is to work backward. How do you want to be remembered? What do you want to be known for? What do you want your kids, family, and friends to think of when your name comes to mind? I didn't want my kids to know me as "hard working dad who was always on the road." Yes, I want my kids to see me working hard, and I want to instill the value of hard work, labor, and discipline in them. I want to recognize the value of investing time in them while they are young. I want eating dinner each night around the table to be the rule not the exception. Is there something particular that you want to be known for? Do you long to be known as the greatest at a particular sport, musical instrument, or industry? The better you define the answer to this question, the closer the answer will be to what you should pursue with your life.

Reflections on the Riches from This Chapter

> Mike Murdock has said, "What bothers you most is an indication of the problem you were created to solve."

> You will realize that your dream is not a thing but is actually the fulfillment and full embodiment of your purpose.

> There is something unique about you that is not common in mankind.

> Live for today and plan for tomorrow.

Chapter 4

MAKE UP YOUR MIND

I s it really your dreams that keep changing or is it the rewards you want and lifestyle you desire to live? To fully understand this, you must first acknowledge that dreams are not things. Dreams are not stuff. Dreams are the full embodiment and fulfillment of the purpose for which you were created. You are not here by accident. Your life is not and was not a mistake. It doesn't matter if you were planned or unplanned, wanted or unwanted; you were created with a destiny in mind.

The fruition and coming to pass of your divine mission is the real dream that lies within each one of us. So it's really not your dreams that keep changing; it's the things that represent the realization of an accomplished dream that changes, and that's okay! I always thought I would buy one particular house when I had a million dollars. But once you have it, things can change. And you're allowed to change the things you want. I wanted a black Jaguar S Type for the longest time. When I had the money to purchase my dream car, I bought a black Jaguar S Type. That was one reward that did not change, but many others have! There are things I thought I wanted, but when I had the cash, I realized that it wasn't really that important to me, or I just didn't want to spend the money on it.

Another phenomenon I've noticed is that it may not be the stuff that I'm associating with success that's changing; it may just be the dates and timeline that I've set for the attainment of those rewards. Life usually doesn't go the way I planned. I hope that doesn't surprise you. I wasn't born with a silver spoon in my mouth or reared in the Rockefeller household. Stocks didn't hit prices I thought they would. They certainly didn't hit those prices in the time frame I expected. Many times, they never hit them at all! I've rarely sold properties in record time. My business revenues never just unexpectedly soared as if I'd hit the jackpot. I've always experienced solid, incremental growth in my businesses, but it's never as fast as I project, anticipate, or desire.

If you aren't careful, this can make you very frustrated. It's easy to get frustrated with your goals and the rewards you've set for yourself. You may even grow to scorn those that have the rewards you've set as a goal. This is very dangerous. Patience, for a dreamer, is one of the hardest things in life to do. Most dreamers would rather walk across a bed of hot coals or walk barefoot over broken glass than just wait. The longer you have to wait, the easier it is to get discouraged. Before you realize it, you might have a defeated spirit. This is especially true the second, third, or fourth time you have to push a date out on a goal that you have set.

I was "supposed" to have my Jag three years before I bought it. I cannot begin to describe to you the late nights, the weekends, the holidays, and other times of great reflection that I sat with my stomach in knots because I had not achieved the goals that would allow me to purchase that reward. It really hurt. I was eating, drinking, sleeping, and living for the attainment of those goals. I was extremely frustrated that I had to keep pushing it out. Of course, there were times I questioned if I would ever be the proud owner of a Jaguar. Yes, I asked if it was meant to be for me and questioned if I was destined to stay in the same economic circumstances for the rest of my life because nothing I did seemed to work out.

I don't know if you've ever felt that way or feel that way now, but I go through periods of time when nothing seems to work out. Every investment seems to stall. If I'm buying, it's a seller's market. If I'm selling, it's a buyer's market. If I'm buying a stock, yesterday was the day to buy. If I'm selling a stock, I should have sold last week. Business sales that were solid simply vanish. I call these times in life dry spells. We all go through valleys. We all go through these dry spells where we don't seem to be gaining ground. We are actually losing ground or fighting to maintain. In some cases, we're taking monumental leaps backward.

I think my expectation comes from keeping successful company and staying around successful people. It took me a long time to understand this, and I still have to keep myself in check, but being successful does not mean that everything goes the way I want it to go. Being successful doesn't mean every deal I do is profitable, every business I buy or build is a great success story, or every stock I buy doubles in value overnight. Being successful is not about conquering the impossible on a daily basis. You may be in the middle of a dry spell and be just as successful as you will be when you're on top of the mountain and have achieved the reward you set for yourself. The only difference is that we don't feel as successful in the valley as we do when we are on the mountaintop.

Let me admonish you not to live your life by how you feel. Feelings are fickle and deceitful and ought to be controlled by you. You are not a product of your environment; you can choose how you want to feel by changing your attitude and outlook. The problem is, many of us enjoy our pity parties. We start feeling like we are the only ones out there fighting for our dreams and paying prices that 99 percent of people would never be willing to pay. We see other successful people around and the jealousy comes out. We say things to ourselves about how unfair it is that we work so much harder than the ultra-successful person, yet we are still sitting in the same lot in life. I once heard that the problem with pity parties is that you're the only one who shows up and no one brings presents!

Everybody is either in a valley, exiting a valley, or getting ready to go into a valley. Life is cyclical. It is not one continuous, joyous mountaintop experience. Therefore, it is incumbent upon each of us to understand that the valleys are a part of it. They are normal. Our circumstances and feelings during this time are not as unique to us as you think. We all feel that way to some degree during the valleys. The key is to be aware of it, change the date on your goal, and start pursuing that new date with passion, determination, and action.

Reflections on the Riches from This Chapter

- Dreams are the full embodiment of the fulfillment of the purpose for which you were created.

- It doesn't matter if you were planned or unplanned, wanted or unwanted; you were created with a destiny in mind.

- Being successful doesn't mean every deal I do is profitable, every business I buy or build is a great success story, or every stock I buy doubles in value overnight.

- The problem with pity parties is that you're the only one that shows up and no one brings presents!

Chapter 5

DO THIS–GET THAT

I'll never forget working with one couple in particular. They were very special to me, and I poured a lot of time, money, and energy into them. I remember driving all night on multiple occasions after being with them just so I could be at work the next day. My goal was to have time to take a shower before going into the office after driving all night. As their mentor, my biggest challenge was teaching them exactly what they must do to reach their dreams in life. Here's the seven-step play-by-play that I gave them.

1. Define your dream.

You build and create your life in your mind. Anything majestic you see was first imagined in the mind and formed with thoughts. So before you can try to reach your dreams, you must first define your dream. I'm not talking about being able to tell me what color interior you want in your dream car or the model aircraft you want for your private jet. I'm talking about a thorough, documented (i.e., written) dream that is aligned with, and is an outgrowth of, your purpose in life.

If my goal is to help one million people keep their dreams in front of them through *iDream,* the online, virtual dream-building site (www.idream247.com), then I begin to define and describe what the finished product should look like. I would then break it down into attainable goals and add rewards that I will get along the way with target dates attached to them. I would not set the first goal at one million dreamers. You set the incremental goals as low or high as you need to in order to realize some success.

As the dreamers grow, so do the rewards. I have toys, diamonds, yachts, planes, estates, and vacations planned, but only when I hit certain benchmarks. Is it possible that I'll blow right past a few? Absolutely. Is it likely that I will have to push some target dates out? Unfortunately, yes. But as I pointed out in the previous chapter, that doesn't make me or you any less successful. In fact, the only reason we ever feel successful in the first place is because we pushed through times when the odds were against us, and we were not experiencing success at that moment. If you experienced successes all the time, then it would become the norm and not a success. You have to define your dream and know what you're going after if you want to stand any chance of attaining it at all. If you aim at nothing, you'll hit it every time.

2. *Write it down.*

If you don't write it down, it's a pipe dream, not a dream. If you don't write it down, you don't truly believe you will achieve it. If you don't write it down, you're just wishing instead of dreaming. Dreaming is not wishing, it's not hoping, and it's not wanting. If it's not written down, then you never truly make it past the first step because writing down your dreams forces you to define them.

When I was in college, I would write and rewrite the facts that I needed to learn to ingrain them in my head. Repetition is the mother of all learning. There is a link and a connection made between your eyes and your mind when it is reading what your own hand is writing. You and I both know that books are more powerful than movies. In fact, many people won't see a movie until first they've read the book. What our eyes see through reading impacts us in a lasting manner unlike most other visual intakes.

This power is further exposed when we read what we write. That's why I had to write the notes I wanted to retain instead of typing them. It was much more convenient to use a computer, but I lost the quality of retention because it wasn't in my own handwriting. When you form the letters and speak the words, it creates belief.

When I was going through the lowest point of my life, which happened to be the lowest economic point as well, I wrote all of my goals, rewards, and dates every day. It wasn't enough for me just to write them once and hang them up around the house and in the car. I had to write and rewrite those goals. I would sit at my desk at work and draw dollar signs on the papers that were before me. I would doodle dollar signs while I was in meetings. It's hard to write and say things that seem worlds away. Write your dreams down now. Break them down into a series of attainable goals. Tie each goal to a reward, even if it's just dinner out, a new tie, or a manicure. Put a date beside them and get to work!

3. Create a plan with specific objectives and timelines.

This is where the rubber really meets the road. There are a lot of people who dream big dreams and may even write them down. But where many people inadvertently fail is when it comes to developing a game plan for how they will achieve those dreams. Dexter Yager has been known to say, "Success is a journey, not a destination." The pleasure of dreaming is in the chase, pursuit, and hunt. Things alone will not make people happy. It is usually the pursuit of those things that they crave, not just the thing itself. Your plan should be a step one, step two, step three approach to how you expect to achieve your dreams.

You need to decide what method you are most comfortable with first. You might start with real estate and end up owning a business. But get started. Take action. I would not be where I am today if I did not start off in a business that had solid mentors that took me under their wing and dedicated themselves to my success. Regardless of your course in life, I would highly recommend you start with a business for additional income and much-needed education. Your leadership and mentor team will be able to customize a plan that includes specific objectives and timelines that are congruent with your life's purpose.

If you have a dream that costs $100,000 and you have established a deadline three months from now to attain it, then the plan should clearly define specific, measurable, and attainable (in sight, but out of reach) action steps that will ensure you hit the mark. There are several ways you could lay out a plan for $100,000 in three months. The method that's right for you depends on your set of competencies. The action steps will obviously vary by the method you choose. It may be realistic for one plan that you get nothing in months one and two and all $100,000 in month three. Another scenario might divide the $100,000 into three equal parts so you have to figure out what you must do to make $33,333 three months in a row. You may decide month one lays the groundwork for months two and three so you will make nothing month one, $50,000 month two, and $50,000 month three.

The next step is to define the actions steps. If I have to

make a big sale to get $100,000 in commission, then I'm going to first define my target customer who is most likely to spend the kind of money that will net me a $100,000 commission. I'd then follow that goal by deciding how and when they should be contacted and so on. If I were going to make the $100,000 buying and selling a house in three months, my first step would be to find the property I want to buy at the price I want to buy it at. Prior to closing, I would already have the contractors take full inventory of what needs to be renovated and establish a timeline, including the scheduling of subcontractors and ordering of necessary materials so that we get started while the ink is still drying from signing the closing docs. Regardless of what your dream is, you need to formulate a plan to achieve that dream with action steps that have deadlines on them.

4. Be accountable to someone.

You must hold yourself accountable. The best way of doing this is to be accountable to someone else. Some people make excuses and say they don't need someone else, but they don't hold themselves accountable. Others put the onus completely on their accountability partner so they can have someone to blame when they fail. If you have both working together, it is far less likely to fail. Most people let themselves off the hook too easily or fail to think creatively in the middle of crisis. That's what a strong accountability partner can help you do. Accountability ensures your resolve and commitment stay strong. Commit to your dream and give it everything you have. It's all or nothing, baby!

My immediate family can attest to the presence of this philosophy in my life. It's feast or famine. I invested every last dime I had and lived as tight as I had to, and still do, depending on what goals and dreams I'm pursuing. I will do today what other men won't so I can do tomorrow what other men can't. I will live like no other so I can live like no other. I'm not holding back. I've closed the back door. There is no Plan B. There is no second string. There is no exit strategy! I'm going the distance. I'm going all the way, and it's all or nothing when it comes to achieving my dreams. I don't want to die with my dreams still in me. I don't want to get to the end of my life and think back on the times I held back. I'm willing to lie in a penniless grave with a smile on my face because I gave my dreams my entire being (heart, finances, effort, thought, focus, etc.). I'm not leaving anything on life's field of battle—no return, no regrets!

5. Take action daily.

Don't make excuses for not taking action daily. I don't make excuses; I don't take excuses. We either do (execute) or we don't (fail to accomplish the mission). We all have imaginary giants in our life. The vast majority of the things people worry about never happen. So why do they spend hours and hours talking to counselors, friends, and family about all of the bad things that can happen and dwell on things that, on a percentage basis, have a small chance of becoming reality? Oftentimes, they feel the full emotional effect that would accompany the horrible circumstance just as if it really happened. What a waste of time and energy!

As a boy growing up in the mountains of West Virginia, I lived in a house with a crawl space underneath. The crawl space was tall enough at the entrance to stand up, but it quickly narrowed to about three feet between the ground and the floor. It was always a bit damp and dark down there. The ground was cold, hardened dirt that was a little clammy from the dampness. There was one utility light that could be plugged in so that you could see, but that just cast scary shadows on everything. I was absolutely terrified, even in junior high, of going underneath the house. I would walk around the house like I was brave, but the second I put the key into the padlock, my imagination would run wild. I heard every scary sound you can possibly imagine. I always thought a vagrant might have gone underneath the house for warmth while it was unlocked and the second I opened the door, I would be confronted with a gun in my face or be kidnapped. I don't know why I was so scared of going underneath the house by myself for so long, but it was a waste of time. It wasn't a real concern. But I felt every emotional experience connected to a kidnapping or worse. I smelled every smell and saw every shadow that would lend any support and credence to my worries. This may be an extreme, but what are you worrying about with just as much fervor?

Worry is code for fear. It's not so much fear of the unknown as it is a fear of the possible. This fear is fueled by the things we watch on TV and news from around the world. Fear of the possible is easier and comes more naturally than belief in the possible. I heard Mark Gorman say that the definition of fear and faith are the same thing: "Believing something will happen that you can't see." Belief requires action and work, which is why most people would rather worry than believe. What consumes you, a worry or your dream?

Stick to the plan you created in step three. Do something every single day that will take you closer to your dreams and the accomplishment of your goals. If people happen to make it past the create-a-plan stage, this is where the next breakdown typically occurs. They are so excited that they have a plan that can get them what they want that they become paralyzed. They just talk about their dreams and how they are going to have this and that and forget or neglect the taking action part. Many people confuse effort for execution. The difference between this way of thinking and the corporate world is that effort is oftentimes rewarded in organizations. In business ownership, customers don't pay for effort; they pay for execution or the creation and delivery of a product or service in a satisfactory manner.

There will be days you don't want to take action on your plan because you are so tired from life. The kids have worn you out, work is out of control, the bills are stacked sky high, and tomorrow doesn't look any better. I heard Mike Murdock say, "Tired eyes rarely see a bright future." If you will take action the next time you don't feel like doing anything, you will notice that the more you do it, the more belief you will have. You will receive a second wind and come alive with energy in the midst of taking action that you did not know before. Don't take a vacation from your dreams. They are worth every ounce of energy and attention you have. Turn the TV off. Get off the couch. Quit playing the video games. Get off the golf course or whatever else is breaking your focus. Do whatever you have to do to stay focused in the pursuit of your dreams.

6. Develop yourself.

I know you want to throw this book at me right about now, but hang with me. Who you are right now and who you have become is what has gotten you where you are. If it's not where you want to be, then you can't stay who you are. Society has really lost hold of this. We should certainly celebrate our individuality, but we should always strive for excellence. It irks me when I hear someone say, "Well, that's just me" or "That's just who I am." We have become a people in love with ourselves! Now is not the time to throw your hands up in the air and throw in the towel because "you are just you and that's all there is to it." No, that's not all there is to it. You can change; you can grow; you can get better.

In my book *Born to be Rich*, I go into great detail about how to change who you are for the better. Most people resist change. Some thrive on it. If you thrive on it, you may thrive on it for the wrong reason. Some initiate change for the sake of change. But I'm talking about growing and developing strategically by choosing what goes into your mind, eyes, and ears. Get your education by investing time with those who are more successful than you are. Books, audio/digital materials, and success conferences have made a tremendous and profound impact on who I am today. This proactive personal development approach, along with the winners that I associate with, forces me to continually get better. There is no finish line for personal development.

7. Keep your dream alive.

At the end of the day, you can have the best plans in the world; you can read personal growth books and have successful friends, but all the planning and effort in the world would be fruitless if you lose the power of your dream. The little variable that makes a big difference as to whether or not you achieve what you want to accomplish is the emphasis and focus you place on keeping your dream alive and in front of you. Dream building attaches tangible rewards to personal accomplishment.

Here are ten specific things you can do to keep your dream alive:

A. Invest time with likeminded people.

We've all heard that birds of a feather flock together. You are, or soon will be, who your friends are. You will pick up their mannerisms. You will pick up their style of speech. You will subconsciously, and perhaps in a subtle manner, begin thinking like they think.

B. Keep it in front of you.

The absolute best way I know to keep your dream alive and well and in front of you is to go dream building. Dream building is when you see, feel, touch, or experience the rewards that you have tied to certain goals in the pursuit of your dreams. They are the objects and things you have chosen to symbolize the accomplishment of your dreams. It may be exotic vacations, luxury estates, private jets, yachts, sports cars, limousines, time with family, golf, clothes, jewelry, or giving time and money to your church or favorite charity. You can make sure your dream stays alive by scheduling time each week for dream building. Nothing beats driving a Ferrari, Lamborghini, or Bentley and actually flying on a private jet from place to place or spending a week on a luxury yacht filled with staff dedicated to your enjoyment.

Most people don't have Ferraris, Lamborghinis, private jets, and luxury yachts that they can just go touch, feel, and experience. To fulfill my dream and purpose, I created *iDream*, www.idream247.com, to provide a virtual dream building experience. I wanted people to be able to go online any time any day to keep their dream in front of them. I want them to choose the features they want in their house or the cars they want to have and the vacations they want to take. I want *iDream* to help you define your rewards. You need to experience life in the mountains and life at the beach and life in other countries.

I used to get frustrated trying to find a big enough house to look at in the town where I lived. There certainly weren't any Bentleys or Lamborghinis driving around! Keep your dream alive by keeping your dream in front of you. Seeing your dream creates belief that it can be yours. The end result of dream building, especially at *iDream,* is that you have much more fun on the journey, and you have the world at your fingertips the moment you feel yourself getting down. You need to go look at your dreams immediately to get your belief back up where it belongs so you can be successful.

C. Take care of yourself.

Taking care of yourself is one of the secrets to keeping your dream alive. When I eat healthy and exercise, I feel absolutely amazing. My body feels like it's at peak performance. It gives me strong endurance and great amounts of energy.

I played basketball all throughout junior high and high school, so I could eat anything I wanted as I grew up and keep my weight in check because of all the exercise from sports.

However, I started to gain weight once I went to college. Since I had to work and pay my own way through college, I no longer exercised. I worked such long hours that it was all I could do to stay awake in class. I even worked a third shift security job to make ends meet and would immediately go to class after being up all night.

Once I got married, my weight skyrocketed. My wife wanted to be a good cook and made all kinds of different recipes. I stayed at that increased level of weight for a couple years before the pounds started piling on again. I started traveling a lot for my job and was always entertaining or being entertained. Multiple lunches and dinners with various appetizers, main courses, and desserts caused the weight to increase dramatically. If there were four of us, I would order three appetizers. From my early days, I felt bad spending $1,000 on food for four people and leaving something on the plate. I sure paid the price for those days.

We finally secured a meeting with the senior vice president of a multibillion dollar, Fortune 100 company. We were all flying in for a three-hour focused meeting. What we couldn't work through in the previous three months, we accomplished in those three hours. We started our time together at a very nice restaurant. As we were accustomed to doing, I started to order multiple appetizers. When I asked him what he wanted, he said he was good with a salad, no appetizers, no desserts. I must have looked at him with a stunned look, but it was at that moment that my world changed. He started talking about how he had run that morning before catching his flight. I felt my food that day was adding pounds with every bite I took. I became disgusted with myself and my body. As I was on the flight back that evening, I determined that if a senior vice president of a major corporation—who was much more successful in the corporate world than I was—could make the time to exercise and make it a priority to eat healthy, then I had no excuse. He was in a higher position and did much more travel, which were the things I used to excuse my weight. Success was literally killing me!

The first class attendant came by at that moment with a dessert tray. For the first time ever in first class, I refused the free food. When I got home that night, I weighed 245 pounds. I didn't wait until Monday rolled around or until after the holidays or even a new year. I started immediately. I would do what I had to do to control my weight. I have lost so much weight over the past several years that people who knew me then hardly recognize me now!

Have you ever noticed that once you become skinnier than people around you, they start worrying that you are becoming "too skinny"? I had people worry that I was becoming too skinny. I never thought I could get below 210 pounds. No matter how healthy I ate or how much I exercised, I couldn't get under 210. We decided to get life insurance around that time. The policy was going to be big, so they had to run a bunch of tests on me. Since my premium was on the line, my weight became that much more important to me. I pushed and worked feverishly to get under 210 because they told me that to get the best rate, I needed to be at or under 207 pounds. The night before I was weighed, I had multiple sweaters and jump suits on while I was jumping rope to shed as much water weight as I possibly could. When I got on the scales for the nurse, I was at 206 pounds. It was a huge breakthrough for me. I leveled off around 209 for the next several months, even though I continued a strict diet and exercise regimen.

Over time, I eventually broke 200, something I thought could never happen. That's when I realized that the closer you get to a goal, the more realistic it seems. Once I broke 210 pounds, 200 suddenly became a possibility. When I was at 245 pounds, I didn't say or expect to lose seventy-plus pounds. I expected to lose twenty. Once I lost twenty pounds, I said, "If I can lose twenty, I can lose just ten more." My first goal was to get under 225. Then I wanted to get under 210. My next goal was to break 200, then 190, then 180.

I am able to be much more successful because of the condition I am in today than where I was a few years ago. I could not have gotten my MBA while working a full-time job, starting a business, writing *Born to be Rich,* actively participating on multiple community board of directors, and being a good husband and father.

To keep your dream alive, it sure helps if you eat right, exercise regularly, and get plenty of sleep. Everybody needs different amounts of sleep to perform at their optimal level, so it's up to each of us to determine how much we need. I know it changes with age, but at this time, I must have nine hours of sleep to be at my best. In fact, if I am speaking at a big event and want to be at my absolute best, I have a sleep and exercise regimen that I will follow. I will let you in on one of the secrets of that regimen. The night before a performance, I purposefully get less sleep than the previous week. I will only let myself sleep seven hours on those nights. I have learned how to ensure I am at my best. Learn what works for you. You need to be aware of your body patterns and how they affect you and those around you. Keep your dream alive by eating right, exercising regularly, and getting the proper amount of rest.

D. Write it down.

Write your dream down over and over again. The more you write it, the more you will define it. The more you define it, the clearer it becomes in your mind, which is what helps propel you toward it. I know it is common advice to write down your goals. It should be common advice to do the same thing with your dreams! It's good to write them down every now and then. It keeps your dream fresh and real in your mind. I find that the dreams come alive within me as I write my dreams out. I begin to feel the emotions as if the dreams were already evident in my life. They become so real inside me that I have to remind myself that I'm not there yet externally. To me, I am already there. But to other people observing my life, I'm not there yet. You are what you think about.

E. Read an inspirational book.

There's nothing like a good book to challenge you in the pursuit of your dreams. There are some great inspirational books that encourage you to dream big and never quit. Those are the type of books you should be reading. When I'm down and I start reading one of these books, I can hardly make it through a chapter without wanting to put the book down and take action. My stomach gets knots in it because I start to get so excited about the future. I know that not only will I continue to live my dream, but my life can be a testimony to others that dreams can and do come true. Years from now, they will see the tangible rewards that I am thinking and dwelling on now.

F. Attend a seminar relating to your purpose and dream.

Every industry and profession has continuing education programs and trade shows. Companies have realized that employees will be more productive in their space with increased knowledge. So they send their employees off to industry-specific seminars and workshops. They may even bring the training in-house. There are workshops and seminars on nearly every topic you can think of, from getting along with other people to creating efficiency, getting organized, and leadership.

Business has realized what most individuals have not: that we respond to education, inspiration, and accountability. If you are used to attending a lot of trade shows and seminars, you have probably noticed that you end up seeing many of the same people at all of these events. There is built-in accountability here. You know they are going to ask how things are going, i.e., sales, performance, life, etc. I always wanted to be further ahead than I was the last time I saw them. I never wanted to go three months and say that things are the same. If things are the same financially and in business, then I wasn't on schedule.

There are a few seminars and conferences that I've attended over the years that really stick out in my mind. One of the conferences came at the absolute worst time and lowest point of my entire life. I couldn't hold my head up, I was so defeated. I withdrew from people and did not want my existence to be recognized or acknowledged. I just wanted to be left alone to work through that difficult time.

I'll never forget my mentor telling me that I needed to go to that conference more than ever because of my circumstances. I told him that my circumstances were exactly why I couldn't go (because I did not have the money), and he said that my circumstances were exactly why I should go! I kept saying, "You don't understand; I don't have the money." He said, "Make the decision you're going, and you will find the money."

That was the craziest thing I ever heard. It was Thursday afternoon, and the conference started the next evening. I lived in Knoxville, Tennessee at the time and the conference was in Tulsa, Oklahoma. He told me that amazing things happen and things come together that ordinarily would not have come together once you make a decision and stick to it. I was in tears on the phone with him that day. I slumped to the kitchen floor (because we had already sold our kitchen table, chairs, and all of our furniture except mattresses) and wept because I was so torn. How in the world could I pull this off? I didn't want to make the decision because I knew there was no way I could get the money. I had already sold everything in my life that had a monetary value. If I could sell my organs and still live, I would have done it at that point.

Over an hour later, I hung up the phone. I was going to the conference. I didn't know how I was going to get there. I didn't know where I was going to sleep when I got there, and I certainly knew I wasn't going to eat for several days. I knew one thing: I was going to the weekend success conference! My mentor connected me with some other folks who were attending the conference, and they graciously agreed to let me ride with them there and back. Two hours later, I was in their van for the all-night drive to the success conference. They knew in advance that I could not help out on the gas, so I made that journey feeling embarrassed, lonely, and dumb. What in the world was I doing? Why did I ever agree to do this? I thought it was the craziest thing in the world I had ever done.

The conference was being held at this immaculate hotel. It was very intimidating even to be in or around a place that had money written all over it. I hated it. I felt like a fish out of water. When I saw my mentor, he said, "I'm glad you came. I believe in you. You're willing to pay the price for success. You're going to do great things." I started to cry all over again. It's hard for an empty bag to stand up straight, and I wanted to just find a chair where no one could see me and just let loose.

He told me he was working on finding a place for me to stay that night. It's really hard to explain to everybody why you're carrying your luggage with you all over the hotel! It's because I was at a hotel and did not have a room and did not know if I would ever have a room. I ended up staying in a room that had several other guys in it.

I don't remember too much about that weekend other than how horrible and awkward I felt, but there is one thing I know for sure. I made a decision that weekend that has stuck with me to this day. I made up my mind at that success conference that it was the poorest I would ever be for the rest of my life. I would never see those people again and be in that financial shape. I had a different attitude on the way home. I thanked the people that let me ride with them as they dropped me off in the early hours of Monday morning. A different man stepped out of their van that day compared to the one that got in that previous Thursday night. You want to keep your dreams alive? Go to success seminars and conferences.

I have a really hard time when people tell me they can't afford to go to things like that. What they mean is that they can't go in style. They can't do it the way they want to do it. They can't fly to the conference and have their own room and eat at the nice restaurants with all the other people. They may have to carpool, and their pride won't let them do it. They may need to pack their lunch instead of going to the restaurant with everybody else, and they aren't willing to do that because of pride.

I looked around at my situation and said that I didn't have anything to be proud about! There was nothing to swallow. I was grateful to everybody for everything, and the mere fact that they would let such an economically-challenged, emotionally-drained social disaster around them was more than I could ask for. I took down the fans in my living room and sold them to pay for that conference. I had already sold the oven and the furniture! I hope you understand why I have such a hard time when people talk about their dreams in a flippant or light-hearted manner. People like that don't see their dreams come true. Then they start thinking that dreams aren't worth dreaming at all because, after all, why should you get your hopes up for nothing? What price are you willing to pay? What cost is too great? How bad do you want it? Where do you draw the line and say that your dreams aren't worth that amount of sacrifice?

For me and my house, there is no line. There is no sacrifice too great or price too high that I'm not willing to die for just to reach my dreams. My dreams will not die in me. You and I only have one life to live. Why not give it all you've got? Why don't you just commit to your dreams before things get as bad as they did for me? I had hundreds of thousands of dollars of debt I had to pay off just to get back to zero dollars, but it didn't matter. I thought about the day I'd have ten million dollars, twenty-five million, one hundred million, and I'd think about how I'd feel when looking back on that day. If I could earn one hundred million dollars, what's an additional $800,000? So if I was already going to do what I had to do to make $100,000,000, I would inadvertently be able to pay off the debt.

So you have a dream. It doesn't matter where you are right now in life. No matter if you're ahead of the game or haven't left the starting gate, you can start today by making the decision to get plugged in to a success conference or seminar that will keep your mind, thoughts, and attitude on the dream that consumes you.

G. Associate rewards to your goals to make your dream tangible.

This really has been one of the most enjoyable and, at the same time, frustrating things I have done to keep my dreams alive. I take the action plan that I create annually and update it as needed throughout the year. I put tangible rewards that are equivalent in value to the goal. When I accomplish the goal, I get the reward. This is what we did with all of the nice things that we have and enjoy. The license plate on my Jaguar is Dream1. The license plate on my wife's Mercedes is Dream2. We've done this with furniture, houses, clothes, and all kinds of other things. We've had many dinners that were goal-based rewards. There were special restaurants that we didn't go to even though we had the money until we reached the goal that was tied to that restaurant. We are willing to delay the gratification of our wants to ensure the attainment of our dreams. Our dreams are worth more than all of the fancy cars, yachts, planes, and homes this world can offer. They are the essence of our very being and are deserving of all our time, effort, energy, finances, and focus. Tie your goals to tangible rewards to keep your dream alive!

H. Take action.

Action creates belief. If the only thing you do in a day is write your dreams down, then you took action. Action stirs up the embers inside of you. It incites the passion that drives you to success. Execution of your goals and deliberately taking action on the plan you have established is what you must do for your dreams to come true. If they are real dreams derived from your purpose, then they will not happen on their own. It will take work, sweat, toil, and labor. There will be long nights and hard times. But you're not counting the cost; you're just paying the price. Aren't you glad there's a price to pay? It's the paying of the price that makes me so proud of my accomplishments once I've realized the dream!

I. Be accountable to a successful mentor who is where you want to be.

You can keep your dream alive by letting other people remind you of who you are and where you are supposed to be. I needed a trusted advisor to look me in the eye during the darkest hours of my life and say, "I believe in you. You're a winner. You are going to do great things." I always challenge and encourage the people I'm around to shoot for their dreams. Go for it. There really is nothing to lose. I ask them about their dreams. A good mentor will keep asking you what you're doing it all for. It's not that they forgot; it's their duty to help you keep your dream alive and in front of you.

J. Create and speak aloud a personal success affirmation daily.

I remember the first success affirmation I ever wrote. Once I was done writing it, I went to the bathroom to say it in front of the mirror. By the way, it is a great thing to look yourself in the eye while you're saying your success affirmation. It lets you see the belief, or lack thereof, in your eyes. It makes you get serious with yourself. All of a sudden you realize this isn't any old game. You can't look yourself in the eye and lie. I sure thought I was in the beginning though.

I said things like, "Rollan, you're a winner." I looked back at myself in the mirror and said, "Well, that's a lie!" I would continue, "I am happy, wealthy, and successful." I'd look myself in the eyes and then down at myself, chuckle, shrug my shoulders, and keep going. "I have been equipped with the power, belief, and strengths to succeed." Well, it sure didn't look like it!

I taped these affirmations everywhere you can imagine. I taped them to the center of my steering wheel so I'd see them on my drive to work. I had them on the bathroom mirror. I had one next to the TV so I would feel bad when it was on that I wasn't taking action to make my dreams come true. We kept one on the fridge. I even taped one to the bottom of the toilet seat and above the commode! I take my success seriously. I am not accidentally successful. Educational institutions learned long ago the power of repetition. Every year I went back to school, the teachers would always review what we learned in the previous grade. It has amazed me to see just how many people practice this in so many areas of their life except toward their dreams.

My family and I recently attended a high school state volleyball championship in West Virginia. My sister was the head coach, and her team had an amazing season. I had just left a book signing for *Born to be Rich* and was headed to catch the championship match. There was a lot of buzz that Saturday afternoon. While they were warming up, the team began to chant. They repeated multiple chants and cheers for a full thirty minutes before the game. I was ready to play just from listening to them! I can't imagine how pumped up they must have been. Those affirmations elevated their level of belief that they could win.

I recently watched the movie *We are Marshall.* I got chill bumps all throughout that movie. Half the team would say, "We are," and the other half would say, "Marshall." They would chant, "We are Marshall. We are Marshall. We are Marshall." Sports figured out a long time ago the power of saying success affirmations out loud.

When I felt like I was lying to myself, I stood in front of the mirror and said, "Rollan, you are a winner" until I believed it. I wasn't going to stop telling myself that I was successful and sharp until I fully believed it. Whether I was a winner at that point or not really didn't matter. I was going to convince myself that I was, and if I wasn't one when I started, I was going to be one before I ended. I am a winner, and you are a winner. Keep your dream alive by repeating success affirmations daily.

Reflections on the Riches from This Chapter

- ☞ If you don't write it down, it's a pipe dream, not a dream.

- ☞ Commit to your dream and give it everything you have.

- ☞ Don't die with your dreams still in you.

- ☞ Fear and faith are the same thing: believing something will happen that you can't see.

- ☞ Tie your goals to tangible rewards to keep your dream alive!

- ☞ Dream building attaches tangible rewards to personal accomplishment.

- ☞ Customers don't pay for effort; they pay for execution.

- ☞ Don't take a vacation from your dreams.

Chapter 6

ONCE UPON A TIME

W hy have dreams gotten the stigma that they aren't real, and they don't come true? Why is Disney World, the most magical place on earth where anything and everything is possible, the only place that we believe dreams can and do come true? One of the reasons people love Disney World so much is because it's what they believed in as a child. Kids believe that anything is possible and that dreams really do come true. Parents love it because it becomes an escape from the rat-race that most of them live in, and they get reacquainted with the dreamer inside of them that used to believe.

We took a family vacation to Disney World one year while I was working. I'll never forget reading an e-mail on my Black-Berry about a crisis back at the office. If I had been in the office that week, I would have been all over it. I would have come home late and spent many hours working on the solution. In that moment, I remember looking around me and then back down at the BlackBerry and just laughing. All of a sudden, it just didn't seem that important anymore. I learned a little more about life and about living in that instant. I looked over at my girls enjoying one of the rides and thought, *This is what it's all about.* Is dreaming cynical? Is it a waste of time? Is it a pipe dream that has no chance of coming true? Not at all. Dreams are real, and dreams do come true.

I've looked at people who talk about their dreams and wondered why they haven't achieved more than they have. I've seen people who appear to be dreamers, yet they never achieve what they're shooting for. They never seem to go anywhere. That is one of the reasons people start to believe that dreams are not real and that they aren't meant to come true.

We all started off believing that dreams do come true, but when life comes at us hard enough, most people derail. The difference between people and trains is that people don't get back on the tracks. They just call it quits. The train company repairs the track and starts running the same route again. Just because the vast majority of people do not live their dream doesn't mean that dreams don't come true. It's that they don't understand how to make their dreams come true. Instead of living in a state of perpetual frustration, they decide to stop dreaming and lower their expectations so that they can feel successful and satisfied. They decide to play it safe.

I remember reading the book by Mason Weaver entitled *The Rope*. He talked about the difference between prisoners and slaves. In a nutshell, if you were inside of a block wall, and there was a rope next to the wall that you could use to escape, what would you do? The book goes on to say (and I'm paraphrasing) that a slave would look at the rope and think, *Why in the world would I ever want to go outside of the wall? Who will protect me out there? Who will feed and clothe me and my family out there? I'm going to stay where I'm at. At least I know what to expect. It's not great, but at least I have the basic necessities. Why should I want for more than that anyway? I'm going to play it safe and not take any chances.*

A prisoner would view that same rope and think, *There's*

nothing in here for me. I have no future here. I belong out there, not in here. The whole world is open to me outside of these walls. I'm tired of people telling me what time to get up (the job). I'm tired of being told when I can go to lunch (the boss). I'm just sick and tired of being sick and tired. The only risk is staying here. Freedom is what I long for. I'd rather be dead than to stay here one more day." The slave saw the rope as a noose, but the prisoner saw the rope as a way of escape. The great American patriot Patrick Henry said, "Give me liberty, or give me death!" So how do you see the rope?

Many people, consciously or subconsciously, view dreams as mystical, intangible, not-meant-to-be-real, mental happy places. That is very different from my world, Disney World, and the worlds of many other successful people who are in the business of turning dreams into reality. If you are aligned and in tune with your life's purpose, then your dreams and desires will be visions of what you are to become, do, and achieve. They are not a place of escape. Dreams are real because they are conceived and nurtured in your mind and thoughts. The more you think and dwell upon your dreams, the more they are being implanted into your subconscious. Your expectation of the accomplishment of those dreams keeps growing and growing.

So why don't everyone's dreams come true? Because it takes belief, work, vision, and sacrifice to make your dreams come true.

Many people have given up on dreaming. They dreamed a dream once upon a time and they did not live happily ever after. Kids believe that anything is possible. We take our girls dream building, and they will ask if we can go ahead and buy the house or whatever we're looking at. My oldest daughter recently asked if I would buy her a real race car. They have no limiting beliefs. They have no inhibition or filtering system that keeps their tangible dreams at the level of their family's means.

You do realize that everything you see or may want is somebody's reality. It has always bothered me when I heard that having a certain lifestyle wasn't realistic. I heard that I should change my expectation so I wouldn't get disappointed. But it was always confusing to me because I knew that somebody was going to live in that house. Somebody was going to drive those cars. Somebody was going to own those private jets and luxury yachts. Someone was going to vacation in those destinations or they wouldn't build places like Atlantis and floating cities with golf courses. What they were really saying is that they didn't think I could experience that lifestyle because it is unfathomable for them. Just because it may not be for them doesn't mean it's not for me.

Most people can remember the days when they dreamed without any inhibition whatsoever. They thought they had the world by the tail and anything was possible. The next phrase I usually hear at that point is, "And then I grew up." If we were honest with ourselves, we would say, "Then our first bill came, and then the job came, and then the house came, and then the children came, and then I realized that it was all I could do to make ends meet, so I chalked my dreams up to a fairy tale that had no chance of coming true."

Some people even become bitter about it. They get bitter at themselves for not accomplishing their dreams. They may just get bitter toward dreaming. They certainly believe that it's a waste of time and energy. I've even heard parents say to kids, "Quit dreaming." They think they are protecting their kids when they say things like that. That is their way of begging their children not to get their hopes up because they don't want them to experience the pains of disappointment that come when you don't reach dreams that you desperately wanted.

I remember working with a family on some dreams they had. They were very resistant to the idea of dreaming. They had dreamed big dreams when they were younger in life and the kids were small, but they never achieved the measure of success they had hoped for. The entire family had been raised in a negative, depressed, cynical, jaded environment.

After a period of time working with them, they started to dream again. They started to say, "What if..." What if I could start a business that would let me be financially free? What if I could pay for my last child's tuition? What if I could be debt free? What if I could pay off my cars and house? What if I could take a vacation? What if I didn't have to work for somebody else? The "what ifs" started to flow. Without even realizing it, they began to dream again. It had been twenty-five plus years since they let themselves dream like this.

Their outlook on life changed. All of a sudden his job wasn't the end; it was the means to an end. Life wasn't as it seemed, it was just a reflection of who he used to be. His wife said it had been years since she had seen him this way. He got the eye of the tiger back in him. He had the heart of a champion, and it was the power of a dream that released it. His energy level shot up. For the first time in a long time, he was passionate about life and about living. Dreams will do that to you.

Reflections on the Riches from This Chapter

- Just because the vast majority of people do not live their dream doesn't mean that dreams don't come true. It's that they don't understand how to make their dreams come true.

- Slaves see the rope as a noose, but prisoners see the rope as a way of escape.

- Everything you see or want is someone's reality.

- If you are aligned and in tune with your life's purpose, then your dreams and desires will be visions of what you are to become, do, and achieve.

Chapter 7

VAPORIZED DREAMS

T he difference between dreaming and daydreaming is belief. Do you believe? If I merely hope something will happen, then I do not believe. If I were to ask you what you want to happen in life and then what you actually think will happen, if the answers are different, then you are daydreaming. Your dreams won't come true, and then you'll think that no dreams come true. You'll think that dreams only come true for the princes, princesses, royalty, and the people who just get lucky. You can have the exact same dream and one day it is a realistic dream, and another day it is a daydream. It all depends on whether or not you truly believe that, not only will it happen, but that it is already done, and now you're just waiting for life to catch up with what you know is your destiny and reality.

Another difference between dreaming and daydreaming is that when you daydream, your mind just wanders. When you dream, it is with intent and takes great amounts of effort and work to control your mind and thoughts. When you dream, it is really an architectural brain-storming session. A daydream is just a haphazard time of directionless wandering by the mind out in la-la land. It usually ends when you hear your name called, and it begins with, "Earth to ... " That is not dreaming. Do not confuse true dreaming with daydreaming.

It is possible that the majority of people innately believe that dreams do come true, but are programmed to view their dreams as daydreams. In this case, they immediately dismiss their dreams and know that there can be no merit or worthiness to them since they did not have to work at developing and creating them. These folks are using the terms dreaming and daydreaming interchangeably, and they are not interchangeable. They are worlds apart. One is a reality, and the other one is a farce. One will come true, and the other one will not. Dreaming is intentional; daydreaming is unintentional. That's why I started *iDream,* not *iDaydream!* I'm not interested in what you hope will happen; I'm interested in what you believe will happen and are willing to make happen. People are willing to pay a price for their dreams that they are not willing to pay for a daydream.

Let me ask you a question. Is dreaming really dreaming or is it merely a recipe for disappointment? Honestly, is it fair to dream? Is it fair to encourage others to dream? How about if we take it a step further. Is it our duty to encourage each other to pursue our dreams, or is it a disservice to inspire those around us to reach down inside and become the greatness within them? Which is it? I have no doubt that there are people whom I've encouraged to pursue their dreams that will not reach their dreams. But it will not be because they can't achieve them; it will be because they weren't willing to pay the price to achieve them. I didn't do them wrong at all. I might have been the closest they came to ever truly believing that they could be everything they secretly hoped they could be.

You are most certain to get discouraged as you are pursuing your dreams. Most people quit the first time they get discouraged or an obstacle comes their way. Tenacious people get back up and keep going. But most people have a limit as to what they will do and the price they are willing to pay to live the life they want to live. How many times do you have to get discouraged before you'll quit? How many bad things have to happen to you in a row before you'll say that it's not worth it and quit pursuing your dreams? Part of becoming a winner is getting to this place over and over and over again and somehow rebounding from it. I don't know how, but you just seem to find a way to put one foot in front of the other. There's no way you can handle anything else, but you just determine to make it through today. You may even set a goal just to make it through the hour, but someway, somehow, you make it through.

I get discouraged from time to time because I don't achieve what I want when I want. But goodness gracious, that doesn't mean I stop dreaming. The goal isn't never to get disappointed. The goal is to get in the end zone! It's to cross the finish line. You owe it to yourself to dream. You are not doing yourself a disservice by dreaming; you only do yourself a disservice if you don't dream! Don't deprive yourself of living life to the fullest and living the lifestyle you were meant to live by dreaming little dreams. Dreams were meant to come true. They are meant to give you a vision of things to come to help you make it through the hard times. So don't stop dreaming when problems and difficulties come; that's when you need to get a bigger dream. Your dream has to be big enough to carry you through whatever you're going through.

Reflections on the Riches from This Chapter

☞ When you dream, it is with intent and takes great amounts of effort and work to control your mind and thoughts.

☞ I'm not interested in what you hope will happen; I'm interested in what you believe will happen and are willing to make happen.

☞ Part of becoming a winner is getting to this place over and over and over again and somehow rebounding from it.

☞ Don't deprive yourself of living life to the fullest and living the lifestyle you were meant to live by dreaming little dreams.

Chapter 8

OUT OF BREATH BEFORE THE FINISH LINE

I was speaking in a college business class a few years ago. One of the students came up to me at the end of the class period and asked, "What if I don't reach my dreams?" I was somewhat surprised by the question because I don't think in that dimension. Not reaching my dreams isn't even an option. My response was something along the lines of, "By when? When's the finish line? When are you done trying to reach your dreams?" I don't know how a person can know that they didn't reach their dreams because I won't stop pursuing my dreams until I'm dead and gone! As long as there's breath in your body, you can reach your dreams! One of the great truths about dreaming is that if you haven't achieved all of your dreams, you get to keep dreaming. You don't have to stop dreaming. Not reaching your dreams should not be an option.

Society has gotten into this mentality that success is a race. It's a matter of who gets to it first. Success is not handed out on a first come, first serve basis. Many people who were once dreamers reached a threshold somewhere along the way where they felt the price was too great and the burden too unbearable and determined that the dream was not worth it. I have met people like this and they say, "I really gave it everything I had.

I gave my business everything I had, and I didn't reach my dreams." Since they are usually saying this in the past tense, I know they have quit trying to make their dreams come true.

The best advice I can give to someone in this situation is to ask this question: "Why did you quit giving it everything you had? You gave it everything you had; what about everything you have?" Every day, every month, and every year, you have more of yourself to give. So why did you quit giving? Was the dream not worth it? Did you get tired of getting knocked down? Did you drop out of the race and get out of the hunt because you weren't realizing as much success as fast as you thought you should have?

There's no such thing as microwave success. If your dream was ever worth dreaming at all, then it warrants your continued focus until the day you're dead and gone. Attach yourself to a worthwhile, lifetime dream that keeps growing and keeps getting bigger the closer you get to it. The reason I want 100,000 subscribers to *iDream* (www.idream247.com) is because that's 100,000 households that are dreaming in a way they have never dreamed before. Once I am empowering and inspiring 100,000 people to pursue their dreams and the things they are passionate about, then my dream will grow to 250,000 dreamers. That is how my dream continues to grow, and the bigger my dream gets, the more fulfilled I become because I'm accomplishing my life's purpose.

I believe that many people confuse the method of achieving their dream with the dream itself. Many families I counsel with quit dreaming when they stopped pursuing one method of reaching that dream. For example, let's say that a goal had been set for the mother of two small children to quit her job and spend the early childhood years at home before they started school. That's certainly a worthy dream to have and can be congruent with your life's purpose, which is to raise fine, upstanding, and honorable children. You may have invested in real estate to make that happen or some stocks or maybe even started a business to accomplish that goal.

Imagine if the real estate didn't go so well or the stocks dipped below the price point you bought them at or the business didn't grow like you thought it would. So you quit the business and you stop investing because you didn't achieve your goal. Do you forsake the dream of staying home with your kids before they go off to school? Do you toss the dream out with the method that failed? The problem may have been the method not the dream.

It's all about finding the right system for you to plug into so that you can execute the recipe for success. Just because you tried something and failed doesn't mean you should forsake the dream. I want you to start dreaming again. I was willing to change the method as many times as I had to in order to reach my dreams. I didn't know what channel would be the best fulfillment of my personal mission. I didn't know if I should just speak to young people or work with kids or write a book or build a business. I struggled with deciding which approach to wealth creation would be the best platform for me to accomplish my life's purpose. That's why I've got real estate, businesses, stocks, and other paper assets today because I tried each of them by themselves at various times in my life. I've gone through several traditional businesses and realized why they were for sale in the first place.

That's when I decided I didn't want what someone else had built. There's a reason they didn't want the business anymore. If it was cash flowing as much as they said for as little effort as they said it would take, they wouldn't have sold it! There is no doubt that I've lost far more money in my time than

I currently have. Let's say you have ten million dollars right now. There are a lot of people who would like to have that ten million dollars. Did you know that most people who have ten million dollars or more have lost much more than that? I've heard Richard Branson talk about all of the money he's lost on different ventures. Sometimes in life the very things you think are doomed for failure become quite successful, and things that should be slam dunks fall flat on their face. Some of the businesses that he thought were no-brainers fizzled before they got started. Others that he didn't think had a chance went on to become industries.

You never know how close you are to the accomplishment of your dream. That's why you can't quit. Success is always around the next corner. You can't stop now. At the moment you quit, you've lost all chances of hitting the home run. You don't even get to bat at that point. You've got to stay in the game to keep swinging.

Babe Ruth is known as the home run king for hitting 714 home runs, but he struck out over 2,000 times. For every one home run he had, he struck out nearly 2.5 times. No one remembers George Herman Ruth for his strikeouts; they only remember him for his home run record. Babe Ruth didn't keep track of how many misses he had; he only counted the number of hits. You may be on the verge of an absolute breakthrough in your business or in your life right now. The night is darkest just before the sun comes up. Now is not the time to stop. If you quit now, you'll just have to start over again. The difference is that you don't get to start back where you left off.

I always thought that I could walk away from pursuing my dreams and come back when I was ready and just pick things back up. Not so. Dreams are not to be trifled with. They are to be taken seriously. When you start and stop, start and stop, you fail to gain real momentum.

It's similar to the law of compounding. What if I told you that you could either choose to take a one-time lump sum of $50,000 or let me pay you one dollar per day compounding daily for thirty days? Which one would you choose? But there's one catch. If you stop any time during the thirty days, you have to start back over at day one and only receive one dollar. Do you realize that one dollar compounded daily would be $536,870,912 thirty days later? Over $536 million dollars would be yours!

You know what most of us do? We get handed $512 on day ten and say to ourselves, "What were you thinking? Why didn't you take the $50,000?" We get frustrated at the snail's pace we seem to be accumulating wealth or reaching our dreams. So we quit. We know that we have to do something to reach our dreams, so we start something else. Only this time, we start back over at day one. So we work and toil and sweat, and we get to day ten only to get the same $512. We've done all of this work and rake in a measly 512 bucks!

This is how most people are living their lives and chasing their dreams. It is characterized by a series of starts and stops. What they fail to realize is that they are going back to day one every time they slow down. If they'd just hang in there a little bit longer, they'd win. If only they had just waited until they got to day twenty, they would have been over $524,000 instead of slowing down at $512.

It's like taking off in an airplane. Did you know that, depending on the length of the trip, most flights consume 90 percent of the fuel they will use during takeoff? It takes most of the fuel to get things off the ground, but once you reach cruising altitude, you can put that puppy on cruise control, throttle back, and just glide to your destination.

Most people never make it off the ground. Their dreams

fail to take flight because they keep stopping halfway down the runway. The effort is not worth it. The price is too great. They've done all this work and only have a few bucks to show for it. They've spent all this money on fuel and look where it's gotten them. They aren't even in the air! I can hear it now, "If this is what it takes just to get off the ground, I'm not willing to put in the effort or keep this pace all the way to my destination." Just because you have $512 after ten days doesn't mean you will have $1,024 after twenty days. That's not how momentum works. And that's not how momentum in your life and business works either.

You must know that your dreams will demand every ounce of energy and wherewithal you can possibly muster. What's more is that it will require that energy and stamina longer than you think you can give it. It will require more than you think you have—of everything! But you can't stop now. You can't quit now. You're too close to getting off the ground. The hardest part is behind you. Don't lose the ground that you've gained so far. If you stop or slow down, you have to start back over. Keep the pedal to the medal and don't let off until you're soaring with the eagles. You were meant to fly. You were destined for greatness. Don't let the bumps on the runway and the frustrations of taking off keep you from reaching cruising altitude.

Reflections on the Riches from This Chapter

- Not reaching your dreams should not be an option.

- You've got to stay in the game to keep swinging.

- Your dreams fail to take flight because you keep stopping halfway down the runway.

- Your dreams will demand every ounce of energy and wherewithal you can possibly muster.

Chapter 9

YOUR DEFINING MOMENT

Peple don't quit dreaming. People certainly suppress their dreams and avoid the things that will stir them up at all cost sometimes, but they don't quit dreaming. There is a seed and spark within every human being that allows them to dream. Depending on how long it has been suppressed, it may take a lot of digging into the cold, dark recesses of one's heart to stir the embers and fan the flame and rekindle that spark of a dream, but it is possible. It is down there.

Why do people quit dreaming? In order to quit dreaming that obviously means that they used to dream. So why did they stop? What was so big, powerful, compelling, or overwhelming that made them give up on their dreams? I'm going to give you twenty-seven reasons over the next two chapters why people quit dreaming. I want you to be on the lookout so you can recognize these pitfalls when they first start to creep into your thoughts and mind. And they will creep in; they don't barge in. They enter in a subtle manner. That's why they are so dangerous. Immediately focus on keeping your dream in front of you the moment you recognize any of these warning signs. Here are twenty-seven reasons people quit pursuing their dreams:

1. They don't want to be disappointed.

More people quit dreaming because they don't want to be disappointed, or disappointed again, than perhaps for any other reason. They have a been-there-done-that attitude. They got their hopes up once, and things didn't happen the way they thought they would or should.

I've had them tell me that if they were guaranteed the win, they would do it, whatever "it" may be. This sentiment reflects a fear of failure. We all have different fears, but fear of failing will keep you from taking any shots at all. From our childhood, we learned that failing is bad and should be avoided at all cost. We were taught in school that we should not make mistakes and were actually penalized when we made them! I am where I am today because I've made a lot of mistakes and kept learning from them. I would not voluntarily make mistakes just for the sake of making mistakes, but they are inescapable if you aggressively chase your dreams.

It is very hard not to get tired of failing. It's much easier just to quit trying. No one likes hitting their head against the wall over and over and over again. So when we experience failure after failure after failure, disappointment and frustration are certain. If you believe in your dream enough, then it doesn't matter how many failures you experience; it's not over until you win. Babe Ruth, Colonel Sanders, and Thomas Edison realized their dreams because they didn't quit after a few failures or a few hundred failures. They experienced thousands of failures, believed in themselves and their product, and refused to quit because they were living their purpose, which made living their dream a reality.

2. It doesn't seem possible.

Some people quit dreaming because it just doesn't seem possible. That's why it's so important that you set goals that are in line with your life's purpose. You can dream and dream big, but it is useless if you don't believe that it is your destiny. You have to believe. The moment you stop believing is the moment you start hoping and wishing. If your dream seems impossible right now, refocus your mind and attention on smaller, specific action steps in the direction of your ultimate dream. This movement will create momentum that increases your level of belief.

There are times now that my ultimate dream seems so far in the distance that it seems I will never make it. I never waiver on whether or not I will eventually be there because I know it is my destiny. That truth alone keeps my belief up. It doesn't matter to me whether or not it seems impossible. It doesn't matter how it looks because that is what it's going to be! I don't just rely on myself and my strength, energy, and abilities. I fully rely on God to make me and build me into the person he needs me to be to fulfill his purpose and will for my life. So when my life's work seems overwhelming and impossible, I simply remember that it's not a pipe dream that I created; it was an innate desire and dream placed within me by the Almighty.

Therefore, regardless of the odds of success or how dire the circumstances may look, the accomplishment of my dream is not about me or for me. It is my duty to work as hard as I possibly can and grow, learn, and improve my skills, talents, and abilities, but in the end, it all comes from him. We have all seen incredibly talented people who did not amount to much in terms of earthly success, and we've seen those we never thought would amount to a hill of beans become immensely successful.

Every worthy accomplishment and success one achieves appears impossible somewhere on the journey. The answer is not to quit. So what do highly successful people do in those times when they feel their goals and dreams are impossible? They just keep doing what they know to do. They just keep moving. It's not a choice. Quitting is not an option because it's what they do and who they are, regardless of the level of success and recognition they may achieve. When you accept your dreams as your mission and destiny, there is a peace and calmness that will carry you through during difficult times without always questioning if you are doing the right thing.

3. They don't want to get hurt.

Many people do not understand the power of the spoken word. Friends and family think they are doing the right thing by warning their loved ones who dream big dreams. This is nothing new. This happened thousands of years ago with Joseph and his brothers. Joseph told his brothers that one day they would bow before him. For the second youngest of twelve sons to say that to the other brothers, those were fighting words! They weren't supportive at all. In fact, they laughed and plotted a way to get rid of the dreamer.

But Joseph knew his destiny. He certainly didn't know everything that would happen on the journey—and it's a good thing he didn't. He might have decided it wasn't worth getting beaten, sold, threatened, lied about, and imprisoned. He might have seen that slavery and prison for something he didn't even do were in his future. He didn't know all of the circumstances he would go through before becoming the prime minister of Egypt. And if he did, he wouldn't have been able to handle it.

It took time and negative circumstances to build and mature the man into the leader he was meant to be. It's going to take some hard times and rough circumstances for you and I to become the people we are destined to be.

I remember when I first started out; I used to tell everyone my dream. I was so excited. I wanted them to see the before-and-after Rollan. If they laughed, it just fueled my determination. If they thought I couldn't do it, it just fired me up and made me want it even worse. I learned a valuable lesson during that time. I learned to keep my mouth shut about my dreams and plans because some people became jealous upon hearing the big dreams. They unintentionally (and some intentionally) began to sabotage my plans because they viewed everything I did as self-serving, even if I was doing something for them! Even today, I closely guard who I share my destiny and dreams with. Your purpose should be well known but your dreams should not.

The reason your closest friends and family, those who love you the most, are often the most critical of your dreams and plans is because they don't want to see you hurt or disappointed. Chasing your dreams will be painful at times because there is a price to pay. But there's a price to pay for everything. You pay a price for failure or for success. The couch potato pays a different price than the athlete, but they both pay a price. It's a matter of which price you want to pay in exchange for what value you receive. The couch potato loses his health, and the athlete must train consistently. One is the price of laziness, and the latter is the price of discipline. The choice is not between paying a price and not paying a price. You pay a price either way.

Relatives and friends are also leery of big dreamers because they know where you came from and may not believe that you will accomplish it. They subconsciously doubt your ability, which is why they want to protect you from getting hurt. If they knew you could do it, they wouldn't be concerned about you getting hurt. You cannot allow the disbelief others have in you to affect your belief in yourself. They also understand that you will grow and things will be different, and they view that as a negative instead of a positive. Personal growth should be encouraged not hindered. Nevertheless, the honest, well-intentioned cautions from close friends and family are among the chief reasons people quit and give up on their dreams.

4. Negative self-talk.

You can talk yourself out of your own dream. The sad truth is that it really isn't your dream to forsake. It was placed within you. We all have nagging, negative thoughts that can talk us into or out of most anything. You get to choose which internal voice you listen to. No matter how much my head might tell me something is impossible, my heart and instinct tell me that I really have no other option if I'm going to stay true to myself.

We each think thousands of negative thoughts a day. Many times, we don't even think we're negative. Most negative people I've met don't think they're being negative when they are being negative! That is because they are comparing themselves to someone who is more negative than they are. To them, if they are more positive than the person next to them, then they are a positive person regardless of how negative they may be.

Being positive doesn't mean you don't understand the potential consequences or turn a blind eye toward destruction or tragedy. I remember hearing the story of an old-time preacher who had a sermon about all the things people shouldn't do. An elderly lady approached him after hearing it and told him he should preach sermons with a positive message. So the next time he preached that sermon, the old-time preacher said, "I'm positive you shouldn't do ... " I don't think that's what she meant, but we need to heed caution about the pitfalls that can hinder our progress.

You need to be very aware and in tune with how you talk to yourself. Do you tell yourself that you can do it or do you tell yourself that you aren't capable or deserving? For whatever reason, it has been very popular lately to cut yourself down instead of other people. So if someone makes a mistake, it's appropriate in many corporate environments for them to say, "I'm a loser." This is usually said in jest or tongue in cheek, but it should still never roll off of your lips. Today's society doesn't understand or value the power of the spoken word as it was in past times.

I knocked something down near an elevator once with a bunch of people looking on. As I straightened it back up with everyone watching, I said with a chuckle and smile on my face, "I'm a loser." Everyone around laughed because they knew— and I knew—that I'm not a loser. They enjoyed hearing a winner say he was a loser when he made a mistake. The moment I said those words, I felt like I had just lied. I felt horrible. I started telling myself repeatedly that I was a winner and that I am not a loser. I could not believe how I felt for calling myself a loser even in jest. Beware of how you talk to yourself internally and with the spoken word. Your mind is a creative workshop and will work to create whatever end you put before it.

5. Unexpected circumstances.

I heard someone once say, "If money can solve it, it's not a problem." That's certainly true if you have money. We all have unexpected circumstances that come into our lives. And the greater success you realize, the greater the magnitude those circumstances are likely to be. When I was poor, an unexpected circumstance was an extra thirty-dollar bill in a month. That would have been an unexpected circumstance that would have thrown any belief I had in my bones out the window. If you don't have full control of your mind, unexpected circumstances can squash your dreams.

I could tell you story after story in my own life where unexpected circumstances nearly derailed me, but I took back control (after I lost control) of my thoughts and mind to stay focused on the dream. My mentor helped me regain control of my thoughts and get focused during a few of those times.

There was a time recently where it just seemed that anything that could go wrong was going wrong. Ever had times in your life like that? I don't just mean one day of things not going your way or a week of things not working out. I had just kept my hand to the plow and kept working and things kept getting worse. Then it hit me all at once. I started reflecting (i.e., thinking; it starts in the mind) about all the things that had not gone my way in the past few weeks. I thought about my rental properties that people had put in their notice and others didn't pay and still others were vacant. We were placing good ads in all the right places, and they weren't working. At the same time, business was down. Not a lot of revenue or activity going on. Some opportunities we were waiting on to come through were stalled. It seemed like there were a lot of things that would change the course of our lives if we just got a little help.

I started to get upset. I said to myself, "After all the work I've done. I've got my MBA. I've written a book that was published; I've been on a book tour. I've started multiple businesses. I own a lot of real estate—things aren't supposed to be happening like this! After all I've done, I deserve for things to go my way. I've worked hard for things to go my way. I haven't relied on luck, but relied on persistence and a power greater than myself to give me favor and pave the way for me to accomplish his will and my dream for my life." Then it hit me. I did this, and I did that. See all of the *I*s up there? Pride. Pride had crept in. Who did I think I was? Just because things weren't working out in my timing and when I thought they should happen doesn't mean that I should quit dreaming big dreams and quit pushing and trying to see them come to pass.

There are people who question if they are doing what they are supposed to be doing or if they are doing the right thing every time something less than ideal happens to them. They blame their dire circumstances on the investment they just made, the business they just started, or whatever they can outside of themselves. Look, if it was the right decision and the right thing to do when you made the decision, then don't question it the first time things get tough. Don't question if you did the right thing and made the right decision just because you have a bunch of things in a row that don't go your way.

Making the right decision doesn't mean everything from there on goes your way. In fact, making the right decision and fulfilling your life's purpose is the surest way to instigate challenging circumstances. Those circumstances come to force you to become the person you must be to accomplish the greater goal and mission of your life. What you know in the light, don't question in dark. If it was the right decision in the good times, stick with it during the hard times. Don't refer to hard times as bad times. Everything that happens to us in life makes us stronger if we allow it to. Circumstances, especially negative ones, mature us. My mother once gave me the following advice during a hard time. She said, "If you get battered and don't get bitter, you'll get better."

Cripple him, and you have a Sir Walter Scott. Lock him in a prison cell, and you have a John Bunyan. Bury him in the snows of Valley Forge, and you have a George Washington. Raise him in abject poverty, and you have an Abraham Lincoln. Strike him down with paralysis, and he becomes Franklin D. Roosevelt. Burn him so severely that the doctors say he'll never walk again, and you have a Glen Cunningham, who set the world's one-mile record in 1934. Deafen him, and you have a Ludwig von Beethoven. Have him or her born black in a society filled with racial discrimination, and you have a Booker T. Washington, a Marian Anderson, a George Washington Carver. Call him a slow learner, "retarded," and write him off as uneducable, and you have an Albert Einstein. It doesn't matter what unexpected circumstances you encounter, winners don't quit when tough times come.

6. Doubt.

Dream stealer number one: doubt. People don't believe they can do it. They don't have it in them. The chances are slim. The odds are against you. Doubt sets in. Why should I pour all of my time, energy, and money into something I won't achieve anyway? Why should I sacrifice when I don't have to for something that maybe I shouldn't even want in the first place? These are dangerous thoughts because they breed a sense of doubt within you. You question if you're good enough. You question if you're worthy. You question if you're coveting and wanting or if it is truly your destiny, and you start to doubt.

You doubt if you can live the good life. You wonder if you should settle for good instead of pursuing great. Just because life is good doesn't mean it's as good as it gets! I've seen good, comfortable lives and lifestyles not get better because they stopped dreaming. They stopped pushing. They retired on their dreams. Sometimes that happens because it was all about things or money. Doubt will steal your dream.

No matter what your current lot is in life, doubt can keep you from moving on. People say to themselves, "I can run this far, but I can't run that far. I can do this, but I can't do that. I can make this amount of money, but there's no way I can make that amount. I can be this, but I could never be that." You can say this sitting in a six-hundred-square-foot apartment in the wrong section of town or a ten-thousand-square-foot country estate, and it has the same effect for both of you. Neither one will move on. The dream for the person in the six-hundred-square-foot apartment in the wrong section of town and the dream for the person in the country estate can both be sidelined and stopped dead in their tracks if doubt takes up residence in their mind.

The battle against doubt is fought in your mind. Your tools to fight the war against doubt are having the right friends, listening to inspirational and educational audio material, reading empowering, soul-stirring books, and finding a mentor.

7. It's easier—path of least resistance.

Why do people quit their dreams? For a number of reasons, but at the end of the day, it's because it's easier. Our human behavior naturally seeks out the path of least resistance. If there is an easier alternative way of accomplishing something, we prefer to take that route. When it comes to the realization of your dream, you have to understand this. It is much easier not to achieve your dreams than it is to achieve them. It takes more self-discipline to pursue and accomplish your dreams than it does to let them die.

Left untouched, dreams die. Dreams are like a garden. Gardens require time, dedication, care, and attention. It's a beautiful thing to watch your dreams grow, but it doesn't just happen. You have to keep the weeds out. Weeds will come in and grow right next to your dreams, but you can't let them wrap themselves around and choke the life and spirit out of your dreams.

8. The dream isn't big enough.

Dreams can die because they aren't big enough. If I lived my whole life for a college degree, and my dream never grew to bigger goals and accomplishments beyond that, my dream would have died the day I walked across that stage, shook the chancellor's hand, and received my diploma. When you start getting close to a goal or dream, make sure that you define a new dream or dream bigger so that doesn't become the end of you as a dreamer.

It's possible for your dream to die because you accomplished the dream and didn't have another one. This can usually be avoided if your dreams are closely aligned with your purpose because there is never an end to your purpose as long as you're alive. You don't ever get to retire from your purpose or your dream. You shouldn't want to! Your retirement date is your deceased date. You don't get vacations from your purpose and your dreams. You don't need one. It's who you are. It's not something you put on; it's a personal mission that is your only ticket to happiness.

9. Undefined dream.

Dreams can die because they aren't clear. They never really were. It's all just a cloud. To most people, dreams are just things. It's the car; it's the house; it's the vacation; it's the lifestyle. Once they get the car, the dream dies because there wasn't much more to it. Once they got the house, the dream dies because that's all there ever was to the dream. It's not very clear. It's certainly not defined, which makes it certainly dead!

If you aim at nothing, you'll hit it every time. If there is no target or the target isn't clear, you'll never really know if you hit where and what you were meant to hit. This happens to people over and over. They aren't really sure what they want to do or be. They wander carelessly from job to job and career to career finding what they can stand or enjoy doing while making ends meet.

We make this mistake with kids as well. We ask them what they want to be when they grow up, and we are looking for them to respond with a particular job. Now, we have to have people who work in all areas of society and someone has to have a job, but we are almost shocked or think they have no drive if they aren't sure by the time they are in high school! It should be the purpose of every young person reading this book, and adult if you haven't yet done so, to search out diligently what you are passionate about in life, determine your purpose in life, and define your dreams that will make the accomplishment of your purpose an exciting journey.

Reflections on the Riches from This Chapter

☞ Doubt doesn't barge in; it creeps in.

☞ If you believe in your dream enough, then it doesn't matter how many failures you experience; it's not over until you win.

☞ If your dream seems impossible right now, refocus your mind and attention on smaller, specific action steps in the direction of your ultimate dream.

☞ Chasing your dreams will be painful at times because there is a price to pay.

Chapter 10

LIFE SUPPORT

Another reason dreams die is because they are shallow. They are covetous wishes and not symbols of an accomplished purpose. Dreams that are tied to things and not substance result in a feeling of emptiness inside. What makes the journey so much fun when you are in the hunt and chase for your dreams is that there's an overarching good that is realized when you accomplish your dreams and purpose. All of a sudden it's not just about you and your success. It's about the lives you will touch and the good that you can do as you realize great success.

10. The dream isn't tied to life's purpose.

I'm going to give you seven questions you can ask yourself to align your dream with your purpose.

    a.   Would you do the same thing and as much of what you do today if you were not paid to do it?

    b.   Will your dreams come true if you accomplish your purpose?

    c.   Did you determine your purpose prior to defining your dream?

    d.   Does the realization of your dream help people outside of yourself?

    e.   Do your dreams support and enhance your purpose in life?

    f.   Are you known for your dreams or your purpose?

    g.   Are you as passionate about your purpose as you are your dream?

These questions help me judge my motives and my heart. For what and whom am I really doing this? If it's for me, then a hollow, shallow, lonely emptiness awaits me. Find a purpose outside of yourself and you will have found a greater calling.

11. Focused on things.

Dreams that are limited to things and stuff eventually die. They certainly die after you've gotten the thing you longed for and had it for a while. The big house becomes the standard, not the dream, after you've lived in it for a while. The nice car becomes the standard and not the dream after you're used to it. It is said a reporter once asked Rockefeller, "How much money is enough?" He answered, "Just a little bit more." Things don't satisfy in the long term. Stuff doesn't ensure lifelong happiness. Dreams that are only focused on things will surely die.

At *iDream* (www.idream247.com), we understand that to accomplish your dream and life's purpose, you should reward yourself for the successes you have along the way with things. You should always have a symbol that you can get excited about that you will get when you hit certain goals along the way.

12. Don't want to pay the price.

This may sound weird, but I didn't want to achieve my dreams unless I paid a huge price. I didn't want to just get lucky or have it handed to me. I wanted to earn it. I wanted to feel worthy of it. I wanted to have that sense of personal accomplishment. It felt good to have sacrificed once I was on the other side of the financial spectrum. I certainly didn't plan on experiencing that sacrificial pain multiple times, but it has helped me relate to everyone I touch.

Life can be hard and lack of finances makes it that much harder. But most people quit the wrong thing to relieve the financial pain. They quit their dreams when they should be quitting their unhealthy eating habits. They quit their dreams when they should quit spending money on clothes, furniture, restaurants, and stuff. They quit the wrong thing to relieve the pressure. They quit the very thing that could get them out of the mess they're in. We know this makes sense intellectually, so why in the world would someone do this? Because it's easier to quit your dream than it is to turn the TV off. It's easier to quit your dream than it is to tell your golfing buddies that you can't go as much as you used to because you're building your business.

I remember telling my golfing buddies that I wasn't going to golf with them as much the following season. We were very close. We played golf every week nine months out of the year and sometimes more. We had a strong routine and finished every round with lunch at a local favorite hot spot. You would have thought I had asked for a divorce when I mentioned that. It was almost sacrilegious to think such a thing, much less say it!

I told my buddy that always rode in the cart with me that I was thinking about taking the six hours each Saturday that I spent golfing and invest it in something else. I told him I didn't want to get to be thirty, forty, or fifty years old and not be where I wanted to be in life and look back at all the time and money I spent every Saturday playing around, goofing off, and having fun. When I'm that age, I will have wished I paid the price so that I can be having fun and doing the things I want at that time. The only thing worse than being broke at forty is being broke at fifty!

I golfed with them a few more times and then kept my word. I decided to replace the time I spent golfing to get my MBA. I erroneously realized that it wasn't an hour-for-hour trade when I was working twenty to twenty-five hours per week on my MBA! I had asked myself this question, "What will I wish I had done that I haven't yet done fifteen years from now?" For me, it was increasing my education. You may answer that question with getting your pilot's license or learning another language or building a business. I had the idea for SAFE School while I was getting my MBA. But even that worthy business did not fulfill my dreams or my life's purpose. I want to inspire others to pursue their dream and pay whatever price they have to because that is the only way to be happy, regardless of where you are on the journey.

13. Too busy.

Dreams often die because we get so busy with life that we fail to work at keeping our dreams alive. We lose focus. We get lost in the trees of life and forget what we could have done with the forest. We build our lives like a really bad architect. We start with a one room house and get married, so we add another room on. Then we have a child, and we add another room on. Then we need an office, so we add another addition to the house. Another couple children later, we have added an additional wing. Have you ever seen a house that has too many additions on it? The roof has multiple colors on it. The paint doesn't exactly blend. The interior doesn't really flow because it's not how you would have designed it if you did it all at once.

Our lives sometimes look like a series of reactions similar to building additions. You've heard the expression that we're too busy making a living that we don't make a life. If you're too busy to dream, then you are too busy. Your life's purpose and the dream within you should determine the direction you move in. Don't just end up doing something with your life. Decide what you should be doing and do it. No one cares about you more than you do, and if you don't take control and responsibility for your life, no one else will either. Your boss isn't going to tell you that you should pursue what you're passionate about in life and your dreams. He's going to tell you not to be late, and don't go home early, and don't take a long vacation, and be available nights, weekends, and holidays, which is all code for "sell your soul to me and the company!"

If your family and your children are a part of your dream, then don't get too busy for them. I have been out of whack in this area before, and it required a conscious decision on my part to not be too busy that I don't realize this part of my dream. We've decided to invest money in housekeepers and lawn care personnel and web designers and staff to help out in the businesses so that I'm not spending all of my time in front of a computer. I don't want my children to come by my casket one day and drop a laptop in so it completes their picture of Dad!

14. It's countercultural to dream.

Dreams are not cool. Dreams are not the "in" thing. They are not in style. The culture says to go to school, make good grades, go to college, choose as high a paying profession as you can stand, and get a job. There is an expected norm in society. If you are going to be a dreamer and raise an army of dreamers, you must understand that it is not going to be second nature.

It's like eating healthy. There's so much junk food at the grocery stores and in restaurants that you have to make the conscious decision multiple times a day not to eat unhealthy food. Dreaming is much the same way. You have to make it a priority to dream. Dreaming has to be important to you so the floaters in life don't steal your dream. Children, teenagers, and adults alike are prone to peer pressure. They don't want to disappoint people. If they dream, they are different. And society frowns on people who are different. They stare at people who don't look like them. They look at people who don't talk like them. Society isn't comfortable with anything or anybody that is outside of what they consider normal and acceptable. Be different—dare to dream.

15. Poor self-image.

Some people let their dreams die because of their self-image. Most people suffer or have suffered from a poor self-image (which, ironically, leads to arrogance). You may believe something is possible in theory, but do not believe that you can achieve it. This poor self image of your skill set or perceived luck leads to an arrogance that anyone with your skill set or below has no chance of achieving that level of greatness. You truly believe that you know what you can and cannot do, and that belief breeds arrogance. This will kill a dream immediately. Many a dream has never even sprouted because it was suppressed at the first thought and attempt at growth.

The feelings of unworthiness come to all of us the bigger we dream and the more we imagine the possibilities. We see what our accomplished dreams look like all at once in that moment. We haven't paid the price and learned the lessons that will allow us to properly handle that with which we've been entrusted, whether it's people's lives or great financial wealth.

One of the sentences in my first affirmation that I said out loud day after day was, "I am fearfully and wonderfully made in the image of God. I am a child of God and joint heirs with Jesus Christ so that I stand to inherit the wealth of God." Let me tell you, if you will say that out loud over and over every day, it doesn't take long before you believe that it is your destiny and duty to become everything you possibly can. If I achieve everything I put my hand to do, then I haven't tried the impossible. I have failed, but that doesn't make me a failure. I'm going to fail in the future, and that won't make me a failure. Don't let a poor self-image keep you from dreaming great dreams.

16. Broken focus.

The one saying I've said more in my life than perhaps any other was given to me by Mike Murdock: "The only reason men fail is broken focus." Entire books have been written on focus, but this statement sums up everything you need to remember. If you failed, it's because you lost your focus somewhere along the line. If you quit dreaming, it's because you lost focus. How can you lose your focus on a dream? You lose focus on a dream when you take your eyes off the prize.

Positive and negative circumstances alike can break your focus. You can achieve an accomplishment or receive a high honor, and it breaks your focus. You rest on your laurels and lose sight of the original prize. Dreams die because of broken focus. Don't look away for even the slightest second. Your dreams are on the line. Don't let success sidetrack you.

I didn't wait to write this book until my first book was a success. It didn't matter whether it was or wasn't because it's the accomplishment of my purpose and dream that trumps everything else. It was my duty to write this book and inspire you to pursue your dreams with every ounce of fiber you have in your being whether or not anyone ever bought the first one or if anyone ever buys this one. What is it that you must do to accomplish your dreams and that requires your undivided attention and focus? Give it everything you've got. Give it everything you've got long before you're successful. It's too late once you're in the spotlight. It's too late to develop the character you need for long term success. It's too late to become the person you always wanted to be. You have to work on you so you are ready when your time comes.

17. Get bored with the dream.

Some dreams die because people have talked about them for so long that they get tired of them. They become old hat. They literally get bored with their own dream. This usually happens because they've centered their dream on a thing instead of around their purpose. They talked about getting a particular car for so long that the model they wanted is now being bought up by first-time teenage drivers.

Dreams get stale and moldy if they aren't nurtured. You have to invest time into keeping your dreams alive. That's why it is so important to build your dreams by looking at what you want. If you don't keep your dream in front of you and keep it fresh, it will die. You know you are bored with your dream when it doesn't excite you like it once did. Your stomach no longer gets in knots with excited butterflies to the point that it's almost painful. You are bored with your dream, and the only cure is to keep the dream in front of you. Find something that will fire you up. Center your dream around your purpose and not on a material object.

18. Rejection.

Many dreams have a short life expectancy because of rejection. The only reason rejection is powerful enough to kill a dream is because people care what other people think about them. So if someone tells them no or that they are crazy or they lose a friend that would rather stay at home and watch TV than to pursue a worthwhile goal in life, they can't handle it. They feel that no dream is worth losing the acceptance of the people they currently associate with. Every time I've moved on or to a different level in life, the good-byes were very difficult because of the great friendships that I developed. I've noticed one thing, though. I've never said good-bye in one place that I wasn't saying hello in another!

Salespeople go through much training in regards to the proper reaction and handling of rejection. I've done a lot of workshops on rejection. We were all created with the innate ability to stand rejection. Our parents told us no, and we asked again. You hear parents tell children no all of the time, and they keep asking. It's as if they didn't hear the answer. Truth is, they didn't hear it because it wasn't the answer they wanted, so they kept at it. You know why they keep asking? They understand that they are not being rejected; it's what they are asking for that is being rejected. People who take rejection personally or think people are rejecting them and not their offer, service, or product are the ones whose dreams die due to rejection.

19. Comparing to other people.

Many an employee thought they were doing great until they saw the paycheck of the person next to them. Comparing yourself to another is never wise. If you're doing better, it's too easy to get filled with pride. If you're doing worse, then it's disappointing and discouraging. Both hurt and both can kill a dream. Pride can keep you from moving on because you think you are doing pretty good as you are, and discouragement can give you the why-try-because-I'll-never-make-it attitude. You might have a dream that has fired you up and kept you going for so long. Then you meet somebody who used to have the same dream, and they tell you about a challenge or circumstance that killed their dream. You might have blown through that circumstance a thousand times, but the next time you experience it, you're going to think about that. It can be equally discouraging to compare yourself to someone who has a lot more than you do. Their success can inspire you in your journey so long as you don't compare yourself to them.

20. Past Successes.

Success can kill your dream. Isn't that odd? It's something to be careful of. It is possible to have a specific dream and get to a place in life that you're comfortable before you reach that dream. This is what is referred to as the comfort zone. We all get in comfort zones from time to time. That's okay. I believe there is a restoration and a renewed focus and energy that comes during these times in our lives.

The danger for many folks is that they never move from there. They settle for what they have instead of what they are destined for. They take the good instead of putting it all on the line for greatness. They tell themselves that they have everything they need without giving any thought to the fact that it's not all about them. That is a selfish way of looking at it. Success, purpose, and destiny aren't all about you having everything you need. It's about you meeting the needs of others.

You see this all the time in business. People start a business and realize a measure of success, but because of how much work it took to get it to that point, they stop. The grand visions of going public or franchising or opening offices around the globe bring on a sense of fatigue at the mere thought of it. Don't let your dreams die because you start seeing some come true. It's just the beginning. Things just get better from here because you grow from the person you are now to become the person capable of achieving great things.

Thinking like a winner doesn't mean that you always win. In fact, thinking like a winner usually means you are an expert on handling defeat! Winners are winners because they learned how to overcome rejection, discouragement, and defeat in sales, sports, fine arts, etc. Thinking like a winner means you understand that it's more than just about winning or losing. It's about chasing your passion, performing at your ultimate peak. Winners don't play not to lose; they play to win. Ultimately, winners aren't even playing to win; they are playing to attain excellence and perfection.

I'll never forget when I played high school basketball; there was one game in particular where we were up by ten points with less than two minutes to go. We knew that the other team was explosive, so when they called a timeout our coach had to make the decision whether we kept playing the way we had or if we switched our strategy to a more conservative approach. Fortunately, we chose to play to win. We stuck with what got us there in the first place and won the game.

That doesn't mean changes shouldn't be made along the way or strategies honed and tweaked. Tiger Woods still makes changes to his game depending on his results, but that is "thinking like a winner." Thinking like a winner means you learn from defeat, discouragement, and failure and use it to improve and do better the next time. Thinking like a loser means you quit; you stop trying. Think like a winner and get back up when life knocks you down.

You may have heard of Harland Sanders, better known as Colonel Sanders, founder of Kentucky Fried Chicken. Harland Sanders created the fast-food sensation Kentucky Fried Chicken in the 1960s. Sanders was already forty years old when he began cooking chicken for customers at his service station in Corbin, Kentucky. Sanders became well known in his home state. Instead of settling down after his statewide success, he began working to take it national. It took him another twenty years before he began franchising Kentucky Fried Chicken restaurants around the country! By 1964, when he sold his stake in the company, the Colonel's chicken was being sold in the company's popular paper buckets at over six hundred outlets nationwide.

You may also remember the white-haired, skinny, bow-tied Orville Redenbacher, who was the folksy TV pitchman for Orville Redenbacher's Gourmet Popping Corn for nearly two decades. Redenbacher was born on a small corn farm in Indiana. He earned an agronomy degree from Purdue University in 1928. Redenbacher had a lifelong interest in popcorn, and while he became rich running a fertilizer company, he also experimented with thousands of corn hybrids, looking for one that would pop up lighter and fluffier than typical popcorn. By the 1960s, he was selling popcorn out of the back of his car. In 1971, he introduced Orville Redenbacher's Gourmet Popping Corn. Once Redenbacher began to appear in television ads for his popcorn, sales went through the roof. Redenbacher ended up selling the company to corporate giant Hunt-Wesson in 1976.

21. Impatience.

Impatience has caused many a dream to wither and die. People want everything now. The credit card industry would not be booming if this were not the case. They want the clothes now. They want the vacations now. They want the toys now. People used to be forced to live within their means. Our world of instant credit allows most anyone to live beyond their means. When we go to restaurants, we want to be seated right away. When we decide we want to be something, we want to do it right away. For the most part, we do what we want to do and when we want to do it.

There's no such thing as microwavable success or instant success. Much of success is waiting. I am constantly waiting on an investment or an opportunity to come through. I have done the work; I have paid the price, and then I wait for decisions to be made or the right buyer or seller to come along. I'm always waiting on something.

Patience will keep you from making rash decisions or investments. If you are impatient for success, then you end up gambling, not investing. Some would argue there is a fine line and motives, intentions, and education have a lot to do with it. If someone has never bought a stock and just started buying the first stock they saw because "the stock market has gone up 10 percent a year on average since its inception," then the argument could be made that they are gambling. Another investor could choose the exact same stock based on company financials, the executive team, and the future of that vertical, and it becomes an investment.

Being patient does not equal doing nothing. I am constantly doing something that will take me closer to my dreams while I'm being patient. I don't stop following up. I don't stop asking questions, making phone calls, sending emails, and staying close to the action. I usually always want things to happen faster than they do. When I'm ready to sell a property, I want someone to buy it right away. When I'm ready to sell a stock, I want a buyer right away. When I buy a house, I want someone who will sell immediately. When I'm renovating a property, I want it renovated right away, without delay or complication. You can be patient without being lazy. If you have been working feverishly toward your dream, don't get impatient and quit. There comes a point in time for every winner where everything seems to fall in line from the work that they have done. Don't get impatient. Find pleasure and take delight in the small successes you have along the way.

22. Past failures.

Past failures can kill a dream. I've worked with people who had a hard time dreaming because of their past failures. They might have had their home foreclosed on at some point in the past. They might have gone through a bankruptcy or divorce or great emotional pain. They may have risked everything and lost everything in the past. They may not have had anything material to lose, but they lost hope and belief—the most devastating loss of all.

Abraham Lincoln lost the state legislature race, failed in business, had a nervous breakdown, was defeated for speaker, lost congressional renomination, was rejected for land officer, was defeated for U.S. Senate, was defeated for the vice president nomination, was again defeated for U.S. Senate, and then became the president of the United States. Where along the line would you have dropped out? When would you have quit trying and say, "It just wasn't meant to be?"

Thomas Edison made over one thousand light bulbs before he made the one that worked. John Wayne spent the majority of his acting career making B and C Westerns until he hit it big with the 1939 Oscar-winning movie *Stagecoach*. Don't let past failures keep you from dreaming and in hot pursuit of your dreams. Thomas Edison reportedly once said, "Many of life's failures are people who did not realize how close they were to success when they gave up."

I grew up in Beaver, West Virginia. I know what you're thinking, and yes, I wear shoes! While I didn't grow up on a farm, I did grow up in a holler. I was a senior in high school when we got our first stoplight in Beaver. Now, I have always loved horses. I worked on a ranch with 110 horses for two summers while I was in high school. In fact, I used to volunteer to muck out stalls just so I could be closer to the horses. I really love horses!

Well, I knew a family that had two horses in West Virginia. One was named Major, and the other was Lilly. Major was a field horse and rarely was ridden, and he didn't particularly care to be ridden either. Major was going to do what Major wanted to do, whether you got on him or not. He liked to do his own thing and was difficult to control, probably was a little crazy! That's the main reason I enjoyed riding him because there was never a boring ride on Major! Lilly was on the other extreme. She had been a trail horse all her life. Her head never came above the tail of the horse in front of her.

I'll never forget the time I convinced my dad to go riding with me. My dad is not what you would consider a horse lover. He had heard many of the stories about Major and had always been reluctant to ride horses. I finally convinced him that Lilly was harmless and if anything, his ride would be uneventful and somewhat boring. We planned the perfect day. We were going to take the horses deep into the woods down to where there was supposed to be a pond. The plan was to tie the horses up while we ate lunch and then begin the journey back. Everything was going as planned. We had a fantastic time exploring the woods, galloping across the open fields, and eating lunch by the beautiful pond in the woods. Major hadn't acted up any more than normal. It was the perfect father-son outing, you know, for a father and son in West Virginia.

Now those of you who know horses know that when they see the barn after a long, hard ride, they like to run like there is no tomorrow back to the barn. We had just exited the woods, Lilly following Major like a good line horse, of course. Since I knew the day was nearly through, and I wanted to impress my dad with my riding ability, I told him to wait at the edge of the clearing while I ran Major across the field, like you see in the movies. With that, I took off. I was digging my boots in Major's side, yelling, "Yah, yah!" I got to the other end of the field in just a few moments. What a great ride!

I turned around to see the proud look on my father's face. Instead of seeing a proud, smiling father, my dad was on the side of Lilly with his shoe stuck in the saddle, barely holding onto the saddle horn and the saddle slowly sliding sideways! Lilly was in a dead run heading straight for the marsh. I immediately spurred Major on to go help him out. Since Major was faster than Lilly, I pulled up next to Lilly where my dad was being dragged through the swamp, grabbed Lilly's reins, and stopped her. Unbelievable! It was the scare of a lifetime. Many people have been trampled in very similar situations. I broke a finger or two trying to stop Lilly, but that was it, no major injuries.

We walked the horses out of the marsh and stopped to rest and collect ourselves. When we finally decided to head back home, I offered to just walk the horses back instead of riding them. My dad said he was fine to ride and got back on Lilly. Now, I don't remember hearing my dad say, "Son, when life knocks you down, get back up again!" and jump back on the horse, but I do remember seeing him pull himself up in those dirty, wet clothes and get back on that horse. Some of life's best lessons are caught more than taught.

When you fail, when you fall, you need to pick yourself off the ground, dust yourself off, and keep on moving. Don't let the failure keep you from trying again. It's okay to fall as long as you fall forward. Winners have failed their way to success. Professional baseball players can fail their way to success. You don't have to bat 1,000 to make millions in the major league. People batting 300 are making millions! That means out of every ten opportunities to hit the ball, they only connect three times! Is it that they get paid millions to miss seven out of ten balls, or do they get paid millions to hit three out of ten balls? They're getting paid based on their successes, not their failures.

23. Don't think it's important or think it doesn't make a difference.

Another trap that will steal your dream is thinking that it doesn't really matter if you accomplish your dream or not. You may start feeling like your dream isn't important or that it doesn't make a difference whether you quit or not. What we often fail to realize is that none of us live unto ourselves. There is always someone somewhere watching our life. What they see will either inspire them or discourage them. Regardless of what your dream is, your pursuit of that dream makes a huge difference in someone's life. It might be in the life of a family member. It may be your persistence has a profound impact on your children's lives.

It is a mistake with devastating consequences to think that your dream is unimportant and doesn't really matter. You might think no one will know if you quit chasing your dreams, but that's not true. You will know, and that's the last person in the world you want to find out! Be proud of the purpose and dream to which you have been called. Do it with all of your might and to the best of your ability. Be the best at whatever you do.

24. Don't have a plan.

Some people stop dreaming because they simply don't know what to do or how they will achieve it. They don't have the vehicle to get them where they need to go. They know what they want and what they should be, but they automatically believe it's impossible because they don't know where to start. You've heard it said that when the student is ready, the teacher will appear. The how of your dream is sometimes not released until the why is discovered. Once your purpose is clear and concise, how you are to accomplish it will be revealed. You will discover it at just the right time. The right business opportunity will come along at the precise moment you are open to it. You will find yourself in the right place at the right time.

I hear stories repeatedly about how people who never do a certain thing or attend certain functions "just happened to go" one time and that's where they met their spouse, business partner, or someone else who made a profound impact on their future success. Don't give up on your dream just because you don't have any idea how you will ever achieve it. Look for ways and means of accomplishing your dreams. You will find what you're looking for.

25. Time consuming.

Some people let their dreams die intentionally because they make the decision that it would take too much time or time they do not have to accomplish their dreams. After all, it takes a lot of time and mental energy to discover your purpose, define your dream, continually clarify your dream, and keep it alive. So they rationalize their dreams away because of how much time it would take. I would agree with them if their dream was merely a material object. But if their dream is tied to their purpose, then it doesn't matter how much time or energy it takes, it is their duty to pursue it. To do otherwise would be a shirking of responsibility and dereliction of duty.

When my dream demands something of me that requires time I currently do not have, I look for areas I can lay something down for the greater good. I gave up golf for a period of time to focus on getting my MBA. I didn't pick it back up when I finished because I found something that was more worthy of my time in protecting children in our schools. So I took the time I was investing in my education and added it to the time I spent building the business. My purpose and dream directed me in a different area, so I started turning over various responsibilities of the business so I could focus on my ultimate dream of inspiring people to live their dream. If I could have kept food on my table and a roof over my head years ago doing this, then I certainly would have done it. But this was my journey. It's what I had to do. Yes, it was time consuming. Yes, I worked on vacations. Yes, my girls put hair ribbons in my hair and makeup on my face while I was starting the business and working on my first book.

There's a lot of talk about priorities, but I believe there is no better way to parent, father, and lead than to set the example. My children see my work ethic. They see the persistence. They see the dedication. They see the self-discipline. They see the same person at home that they do on a stage speaking to thousands of people passionate about pursuing their dreams.

26. Don't want to commit or be accountable for it.

Some people stop dreaming because they don't want to commit or be accountable for the results. It's really because they don't ever want to feel like they failed. They can live with themselves if they never achieve their goal because they never really committed. They never feel bad about their performance because they never really sold out to begin with. Don't let this fear or a potential feeling of guilt that you didn't measure up compared to other folks who made the levels you were shooting for keep you from dreaming. It's just not worth it. We only have one life to live, and if your dream is an offshoot of your purpose, then you can logically give your purpose and dream absolutely everything you have. Your job is to give yourself wholly to your purpose and dream regardless of the cost.

Life is a lot like school. You have one kid who never picks the book up and makes straight As, and you have another kid who studies for hours night after night and makes a B if they're lucky. How does that feel? How fair is that? It's really not about that. It's about each individual person performing at the highest and greatest level they can. It is possible for the kid that is naturally an A-student to be worse off than the B-student that studies and works hard because the B-student is performing to his potential, and the A-student may be capable of much more if they'd only put forth the effort.

27. Not enough self-discipline.

Being successful and realizing your dreams takes hard work. It doesn't happen just sitting around. In addition to a lack of respect for authority and a lack of appreciation for freedom, hard work, and the value of the dollar, many of today's generation lacks self-discipline as a whole. It's all about what they want to do with no regard to commit. A sense of duty is not understood by many in my generation and today's generation. If there's a commitment and something else comes up that they'd rather do, they don't think twice about blowing the commitment off or rescheduling.

A lack of self-discipline can be seen in the stomachs of a vast majority of Americans. Our waistlines are almost as big as our debt. In historic times, obesity was tied to wealthy people because they could afford all of the food. In modern times, obesity is tied to poverty because healthy food is expensive and the food provided from government assistance and fast food restaurants, by and large, is not. It takes a lot of self-discipline to stay away from all of the unhealthy food that surrounds us in vending machines, restaurants, parties, holidays, schools, and the work place. I was amazed at all of the cupcakes and unhealthy eating that takes place every time a kid in my daughter's class at school has a birthday. She's having cake every week!

We work very hard not to celebrate with unhealthy food. For example, we do not use ice cream as a reward. I'd rather take that dollar and let them pick out something from the dollar store than spend it on junk food. We used to always celebrate by going out to dinner. Every time we had a success worthy of celebration, out to eat we'd go. And the only thing that separated it from all of the other times we went out to eat was that we would order dessert. We eventually linked success with unhealthy eating. That is a dangerous precedent that I did not want to establish for my girls or myself.

To do anything successful in life, it requires a high level of personal discipline. The most successful athletes spend hours, months, and years training for us to marvel at their skill for just a few moments. A great pianist once said that if he didn't practice for a day, he could tell the difference. If he went two days without practicing, his family knew it. If he went a week without practicing, everyone else could tell.

No matter what your purpose, dream, and calling, it will require self-discipline. Delaying things that satisfy yourself until you accomplish a set goal is a triumphant feeling. Delayed gratification encourages self-discipline because that's the only way you will accomplish the victory you're working toward. Get your life organized, disciplined, and stick to the schedule. Bosses were invented for people who couldn't get to work on time and wouldn't work if they didn't have somebody standing over them with a verbal whip and three-strikes-you're-out policy. You should be harder on yourself and hold yourself to a higher level of personal discipline than a boss or company ever could. You aren't average nor should average be the standard. Excellence is the standard.

Reflections on the Riches from This Chapter

☞ Fully rely on God to make you and build you into the person he needs you to be to fulfill his purpose and will in your life.

☞ Every worthy accomplishment and success one achieves appears impossible somewhere on the journey.

☞ When you accept your dreams as your mission and destiny, there is a peace and calmness that will carry you through during difficult times without always questioning if you are doing the right thing.

☞ Your purpose should be well known, but your dreams should not.

☞ What you know in the light, don't question in dark. If it was the right decision in the good times, stick with it during the hard times.

☞ If you get battered and don't get bitter, you'll get better!

☞ Center your dream around your purpose and not on a material object.

☞ Thinking like a winner doesn't mean that you always win.

☞ Much of success is waiting. Be patient without being lazy!

☞ To do anything successful in life, it requires a high level of personal discipline.

Chapter 11

MAKING YOUR DREAMS COME TRUE

S o you have this dream. You want it more than anything else. It's the purpose and mission of your life. What now? How do you make your dreams come true? Dreams come true by developing as a person, working diligently and consistently, maintaining the right spirit, heart, and mind by controlling your thoughts, giving everything to it that you have been given, and in time.

You see, you have been given all of the tools, connections, and finances you need to accomplish the next step and take you to the next phase of your dream. It is in your life at this moment. Your mission is to discover these things that are currently present in your life.

Belief and persistence have helped many a dreamer live their dreams. They just kept knocking; they just kept asking. They didn't quit. They won because they were the last one standing. They were the only one left. When everyone else was quitting, they put a stake in the ground and refused to give up the ground they had taken. You have to believe in yourself. You have to believe in your dream. You have to believe in your cause, and you have to believe that your success is not rooted in yourself but is the culmination of other people in your life and the Almighty working in you to accomplish his will. You must believe that all things are possible if you are called to do them. There are a lot of things that are impossible to me that are possible to someone whose mission it represents. It's impossible for me to compete in the NBA, but it is more than possible—it is reality—for those that are in the NBA.

Dreams do come true. Disney World is a classic story of belief. The dreamer, Walt Disney, along with his brother Roy, launched their business with a wild-hair idea. They wanted to create a magical place that inspired people of all ages to believe their dreams could come true. They saw how much fun people were having when the fair came to town and wanted to create a permanent fair eventually known as an amusement park. Investors told him he was crazy, and his idea would not work. Nobody would come. People come from all over the world today, but it was Walt Disney's belief in his dream, hard work, persistence, and determination in spite of rejection and seemingly insurmountable odds that brought forth what we experience today.

If you were to ask a sports star, movie star, or musician what it took to make it to the major leagues or hit the big time, they would probably have an answer similar to what made Walt Disney successful. They would say they had an idea that they believed in, worked hard, were persistent in the face of adversity, and were determined to keep trying no matter how many times they were rejected and no matter the odds because they had nothing to lose no matter what they had. If you don't have your dreams to chase, then you really don't have anything at all.

I've heard relatives of people at the end of their lives say that their loved one died because they lost the will to live. This is often true, but I'm afraid it happens before the physical death more times than not. There are people dying every day that haven't lived in years. They lost hope a long time ago. They gave up on their dreams long ago. They gave up on discovering their purpose and living their life according to that purpose years before. If you are breathing, you can live and pursue your purpose with a fierce and fiery passion. There are people who cannot read the words on this page that have every opportunity for great success because they believe in their dream, don't know the meaning of the word no, and have the persistence, determination, and will never to quit.

A requirement for success isn't higher education. A requirement for success isn't that you come from a family of means, wealth, and prominence. A requirement for success isn't that you do something that no one else can do. You can be successful and have all of your dreams come true by believing in your dream, believing that you have been equipped by the Almighty to accomplish it, refusing to quit or give up, working hard, and doing your dead-level best at what you've been called to do, no matter how minor or unimportant it may seem.

If you are doing these things, then your mind is in the right place. You're thinking the right thoughts and controlling your mind. If you are having a difficult time believing that you can achieve your dream, you need to go to work on your thought life. The battle for your life is fought in your mind. Be a defender and a champion of your dream. If you don't fight for it, no one else will. I can't accomplish your dreams for you. Only you can do that. You can't accomplish my dreams for me. Only I can do that. But we can work together to help both of us achieve our dreams. Dreams were made to come true. They weren't designed by the Creator to drive you nuts, get you frustrated, or leave you feeling empty and like a failure. You have the seeds of greatness in you, along with everything you need to move your dream forward in your life right now.

Reflections on the Riches from This Chapter

- Dreams come true by developing as a person, working diligently and consistently, maintaining the right spirit, heart, and mind by controlling your thoughts, giving everything to it that you have been given, and in time.

- Belief and persistence have helped many a dreamer live their dreams.

- You have to believe in your cause, and you have to believe that your success is not rooted in yourself, but is the culmination of other people in your life and the Almighty working in you to accomplish his will.

- There are people who cannot read the words on this page that have every opportunity for great success because they believe in their dream, don't know the meaning of the word no, and have the persistence, determination, and will never to quit.

Chapter 12

KEEPING THE DREAM ALIVE

D reams come alive with realistic plans. Realistic plans create a belief and enthusiasm that you will live your dream. With each level of success you achieve on your plan, you should attach a tangible symbol of the accomplishment of that dream. You may attach your dream car to one of your goals. You can attach lavish vacations, homes, planes, yachts, motor coaches, clothes, cosmetic surgery, jewelry, hobbies, or giving to various goals. But it is vitally important that you find something that you want in conjunction with your dream and purpose. It keeps the dream alive. It takes the intangible and makes it tangible. What we see affects our belief, so it monetizes the success and dreams we have.

We've all heard people say, "I'll believe it when I see it." This is true in many areas. Our minds take what we see to elevate our level of belief. I have noticed that if I found something I wanted bad enough, I was willing to do things I wouldn't ordinarily do for it. For example, my dream and purpose is to inspire others to pursue their dreams no matter the cost. That's a great purpose and a worthwhile dream, but it may not be enough to get me off the golf course or off the couch from a good college football game. I have to find something that I can attach to each goal that I've created to accomplish my purpose and assign something I want bad enough to get me to take action.

I change the objects and symbols that are beside my goals from time to time. The more I browse www.idream247.com and the more I hear, see, and experience the dreams of others, the more I see that there is so much more than I ever imagined. The possibilities are endless. If you have a specific car that you have assigned to a particular goal, you need to do everything you can to drive it so you know what color you want, what it feels like to sit in the driver seat and start the car, how the car idles, what the steering wheel feels like when you grip it, and how it turns. You need to know what it smells like so you can be sitting at home and still smell it when you want to. You need to look at your specific dream online to keep it in front of you. You need to find something that you can get excited about that will encourage you to make the next phone call, send the next e-mail, go to the next success conference, read the next book, listen to the next audio, close the next deal, and become fear and rejection proof.

We drive through the nicest neighborhoods we can find. We drive the nicest cars we can. We get tours of the most lavish hotels that we can. We try on fancy clothes. We spend hours and hours going through the pictures on www.idream247.com and defining what we like and don't like so we know exactly what we want. We invest a lot of time in defining the specific rewards that we attach to our goals because it fires me up. It keeps me focused. It keeps my master dream alive! I know it's time to stop when my stomach can't handle it anymore. I get so excited and nervous that I can't stand it. I just want to take action right away.

Can you imagine pulling up to your house with massive gates, pushing a button and watching the gates open, and then driving up the long, winding, tree-lined driveway? Can you imagine looking out your window on the way up to your house and seeing the runway for your private jet? Can you see your hundred-foot yacht moored at the edge of your waterfront home? I can imagine a helipad with a helicopter sitting next to the hangar. You finally round the last turn in your driveway to behold the most breathtaking country estate with a Mediterranean flair you have ever seen.

I can see the indoor pool extending underneath a panel of glass to the exterior infinity edge pool that contains the ending of a hundred-foot water slide, and the rolling green lawn just beyond it that extends out to the water. I can see the three-hole golf course that wraps around the hangar and winds around multiple guesthouses in between the main house and the water. I see mules, golf carts, four-wheelers, snowmobiles, and other all-terrain vehicles being utilized by friends and family. I can see several horses grazing in the lush pastures.

You then pull your car into the ten-car garage. As you enter the main house, you gasp at the grandness and magnitude of the foyer, dual-winding staircase, and waterfall with the most beautiful view of the water through the multilevel glass wall. Can you imagine having a home with elevators in it? Can you imagine deciding to go bowling and the family heads downstairs? Can you imagine a trip to the gym meaning that you're going to the west wing of the house? Can you see a multiplatform home theatre with a full stage and screen for home theatrical plays and watching TV? That has to be the best Super Bowl party ever! Wouldn't that be the best way to watch college football? Your reward can be whatever you want it to be. It's whatever you want to make it. You may not want anything like this or already have this, but that doesn't matter. The point is that you need to define and continue clarifying and exploring tangible symbols that you can attach to your goals.

Reflections on the Riches from This Chapter

☞ With each level of success you achieve on your plan, you should attach a tangible symbol of the accomplishment of that dream. Belief and persistence have helped many a dreamer live their dreams.

☞ You need to find something that you can get excited about that will encourage you to make the next phone call, send the next e-mail, go to the next success conference, read the next book, listen to the next audio, close the next deal, and become fear and rejection proof.

☞ Continue to define, clarify, and explore tangible symbols that you can attach to your goals.

Chapter 13

THE REALITY OF REALITY

Dreams are real. It is not some mystical place in one's imagination in the land of make-believe. Dreams are merely thoughts about what you want your future to look like. Thoughts are the only tangible things from which anything has ever been created. Before a building can be built, it must first be imagined in someone's mind. Before words are written or spoken, they must first pass through the mind. Machines, houses, cars, clothes, phones, computers, businesses, the stock market, even the world itself was first a thought. What is in the heart and mind of mankind will soon be reflected on the outside. This is the role and purpose of the mind. It serves as a data repository. It doesn't judge whether the input is accurate, true, positive, or negative; it just processes and stores what comes in. Your future is determined by what is put in.

If you are a gymnast and you eat, sleep, and breathe gymnastics, then that is what you will eventually become. What you dwell on and what you pour yourself into the most will win. That is who you will become. As you know, most people just think whatever thoughts they happen to think. They think about the news they hear, but they didn't choose to listen, think, or process that kind of information, they just did it. They think about the conversations that are brought up at work without giving any real thought to designing their future by channeling their thoughts.

Thoughts are real. We all know there are such things as thoughts. Proverbs says, "As a man thinketh in his heart, so is he." You are, or soon will be, what you think about. Back in the 1990s, there was a slogan that said, "You are what you eat." That's true, but I'm just as concerned that you are what you think! Since thought is the only real and tangible thing from which anything is created and dreams are simply a string of real and tangible, positive thoughts, your dreams can come true if that is what you keep before your mind's eye. That's why dream building is so important. The eyes affect the mind. Seeing is believing. The more you see, touch, feel, and experience your dream, the more your mind will dwell on it and lead you to the resources necessary to accomplish it.

We go through life manifesting our thoughts. The actions we take and the words we speak are the projection of our mind and thoughts. If actions are a result of what we think in our minds, and we are and will become what we think about, then our reality is not the external world we live in, but is the internal world in which we dwell. Your reality is not the house you live in, the car you drive, and the vacations you take. Those are the tangible reflections of your actual reality that is found in your mind. Where you are is who you were. Who you become depends on what you think about now. The phrase "perception is reality" is true because perceptions are created in your mind and what you think is your real reality, not the physical world we operate in.

I drove my Jaguar a long time before I purchased it. My body might have been in a Ford Explorer, but I felt the Jaguar steering wheel. I smelled the interior. I knew where the temperature and volume controls were on the Jaguar, and they were in the wrong place for a while (because my body was in a different place than my reality). I lived in a different house long before I got it. This truth is one of the main ways that I stay content with what I have been given. I'm always thankful for what I have because I have what I'm destined for at the moment I accept full responsibility for that vision and commit to it. It's mine. It's as good as done. I'm so thankful because that is where I'm living and what I'm driving even though my body and family do not get to reap the benefits of those pleasures yet.

Your dreams can be your reality if that is what consumes you. So what is your reality? Your tangible, physical environment may be your reality if you don't control your thoughts and just think about whatever you happen to think about. I don't want to live where I am; I want to live where I'm supposed to be. I want to live in the land that's been promised to me. I want to live the life that the fulfillment of my purpose allows me to live. I don't have to wait until I write the check for the house, the car, the plane, the yacht, the business, or whatever it is for it to become my reality. It already is my reality!

If I took your thoughts for the last month and played it back on a movie screen for all to view, what would we see? Would I be able to tell you exactly what your dream and purpose in life is? Would I find that your reality is not what I see on the outside? You get to choose where you live because we live in a world of thought. We operate and exist in a physical world, but we live in the thought world. So where do you live? Who are you? What are you becoming? What does your life look like? You can live your dreams now by dwelling on your dreams in your thoughts and mind.

Reflections on the Riches from This Chapter

- What is in the heart and mind of mankind will soon be reflected on the outside.

- Since thought is the only real and tangible thing from which anything is created and dreams are simply a string of real and tangible, positive thoughts, your dreams can come true if that is what you keep before your mind's eye.

- The more you see, touch, feel, and experience your dream, the more your mind will dwell on it and lead you to the resources necessary to accomplish it.

- Where you are is who you were.

Chapter 14

COST DOESN'T MATTER

I s it worth giving every last cent to the fulfillment of your dreams with no guarantees on when you will accomplish your purpose? Is it worth giving every waking moment to your dream? Is your dream worth one hundred percent of your focus, time, and energy? Will you look back thirty, forty, fifty years from now and wish you had not sacrificed quite so much for your dreams or will you look back and wish you had done more? There comes a point in all of our lives where we look back and say, "I'm glad I did" or "I wish I had."

Now, I've heard plenty of people say I wish I hadn't spent so many hours on the job or in the office. I've heard many a business traveler say they wish they had invested more time with their children. The regrets they have are over missed ball games, recitals, and school programs. They didn't see their child score their first basket or they missed the first home run. When the child looked into the stands for the approval and recognition they longed for, dad or mom wasn't there. There is a vast difference between giving your dream and purpose everything you are and have in life and giving the same to your job. One will leave you full of regrets while giving yourself entirely to the cause of your dream and purpose will leave you fulfilled, and your children will be proud of your drive, dedication, and passion. You will inspire your family and everyone you touch.

It is not a fair or accurate comparison to judge what you are willing to do for your job with what you should do for your dream and purpose. It is expected that you do much more for your dream and purpose than you would ever do for your job. I would not miss a holiday with my family for my job, but I would do what I had to do if it were for my dream and purpose. I'm setting the tone and expectation that there are some things in life that are worth giving our all to. I will do today what other men won't (give up a holiday) so I can do tomorrow what other men can't (spend all week with the family). I'm willing to give up a holiday to pursue my dreams if I can't arrange it otherwise so I can spend all week with them while everyone else is at work.

There are many more people who understand and practice this than we realize. You'll see news commentators host parades every year on Thanksgiving and Christmas. They are working on a holiday for their job, but for many of them, that is their dream. It's not work at all. Think about all of the football and basketball games. All of those players chose to play football or basketball instead of staying at home, watching TV, eating ham and turkey, opening presents, and having a standard Christmas like everyone else. They aren't spending those holidays at their parents' house or in another part of the world. Their dream requires their presence so that they can continue to fulfill what they are meant to do. No one is at home feeling sorry for those poor individuals having to work on a holiday.

Why don't we feel bad for them, but we feel bad for people who have to work their job on a holiday instead of spending it with friends and family? It's because we realize that it's their passion and there's probably nothing they'd rather be doing to celebrate a holiday than doing what they love. We don't view it as their work; we view it as their dream—and it probably is.

So what's your dream? Is your dream worth working on a holiday? Of course, you won't view it as working because it's your dream. If you like what you do, you'll never work a day in your life. Two people can be doing the exact same job or function, and one person loves it and the next person hates it. It doesn't feel like work to the person who loves what they do, but it epitomizes work and is painful to the person who doesn't like it. If your dream is work to you, then you may need to have a check-up to make sure your dream is aligned with your purpose.

I don't feel like I'm working when I speak because that's when I'm living my dream. I don't feel like I'm working when I'm writing because I enjoy sharing my thoughts and inspiring other people. To anyone who is watching me spend hour after hour, week after week, month after month, and year after year pursuing my dreams, it most definitely appears like work. And if I didn't love it, it would be work. It seems like a hobby that I'm just very dedicated to. No one has to tell me to work on my dream today. I want to work on my dream. No one has to tell me what needs to be done next for my dream because it's all I think about. It consumes me.

Whether or not other people see the dreams that I dream or the visual, physical result of my dreams is not as important to me as it is that I keep dreaming. I never feel more alive than when I'm chasing my dreams. Just because I don't have every tangible reward I've set next to some great goals doesn't mean that I'm not living my dream. My dream doesn't have a dead-line on it. My dream doesn't have an expiration date. It's not something that I can attain and then stop. It is my life's purpose. It is my mission in life. It is my passion. The results aren't up to me. It's up to me to do and be and become all that I can.

Yet, I can't get to where I want and need to be on my own. I need favor. I need favor in the sight of God and man. I need people to invest in my dream. I need mentors who will take me under their wing and invest time and energy into me. I need encouragers and fans to keep me inspired and focused on the journey. I need to achieve great accomplishments and receive recognition on the journey, and I can't do any of these things by myself. They require favor. Someone, somewhere, at some point in time needs to say, "I've been waiting for some-one like him to come along all my life. That's my protégé, and he doesn't even know it yet. That boy right there, yes you, you are going to run my multimillion-dollar business. I've been waiting for someone I could pour my life's work, wisdom, and finances into that would make an impact for the good of humanity."

Is your dream worth it? Is it worth it to give your dream everything you have? What if you've dreamed for years and don't have much to show for it; is it still worth it? Is it still worth sacrificing for, or should you take some of that money and time and pick up a sport, join the country club, or start traveling?

It's worth it, my friend. It's worth everything you've got and everything you're going to get. It's worth any amount of extra time, money, and energy you can invest into it. It's not about you. Your dream is not merely so you can have an unbe-lievable lifestyle. You weren't created for you, and no man lives unto himself. There's a plan for your life. Your life has a pur-pose and meaning. You are valuable and precious. Your success is not measured by what you accumulate on earth, but by how you fulfilled the purpose for which you were created.

Even if I never get the car of my dreams or the house of my dreams or got to travel, see the world, fly on private planes, and cruise on luxury yachts, just the fact that I'm shooting for my dreams excites me. The thought that tomorrow will be better than today is enough to fire me up. I know that I am doing absolutely everything I possibly can to achieve my dreams and purpose right now. When you can say that, then you are touching and influencing everyone that you are supposed to at that time.

I want to influence more people to pursue their passion and not a paycheck or a pension. I want to inspire more people to chase their dreams, not money. We've got it all backward. We go to work to make a living because we waited too long before we started making a life. Start today making your life by making the decision that your dreams are worth it.

Realize that your dreams aren't just your dreams. You were given desires, wants, and dreams that would empower you to pursue your purpose with singleness of mind. Those aren't your dreams at all. Those dreams have been given to you because you are the only one who can make them come true. I wasn't given the same dreams and desires as you because I can't make them come true. I can only make my dreams come true. If you don't make your dreams come true, who will? There's nothing more worthy, noble, and upstanding that you can do with your life than chase your passion and follow your dream. A country can expect nothing more from its citizens than for each one to pursue their dreams with hard work, integrity, persistence, and unwavering belief.

I have never doubted what my dream and purpose is, but I have doubted if I will ever be able to see it and touch it. That's when I realized that seeing it and touching it is not the point. I can live my dream long before I can touch my dream. I can live in my dream house long before it is constructed because my reality is what I think about. We live in our minds and in a thought world. The point of dreams is not just to see them come true; did you know that? The point of dreams is to keep us excited on our journey as we fulfill our purpose. Dreams are the fuel. Dreams keep the fire lit and hot. Dreams wake us up in the morning and keep us up late at night. We do it for the dream.

Your time is coming. Dream big dreams. There is a brighter day ahead. There is light at the end of the tunnel. No valley lasts forever. It doesn't rain in the same spot continually. The sun eventually comes out. There is a pot of gold at the end of your rainbow. But it doesn't just happen. You don't get there because you are you. You don't get there just because you have the dream. You get there because you paid the price. You stayed focused on the course and the task at hand. You kept your dream alive and always believed in your dream and purpose.

If I'm going to lose everything I've got, I want it to be because I was chasing my dream, not because I was greedy. You don't hear too many people on their deathbed say they wished they hadn't given their life and dreams all they had. You usually hear how much they regret not maximizing their time and giving more of themselves to their purpose, dreams, and to others. At the end of the day, dreams are not about what you have or don't have; it's about who you become as you move toward a dream that is bigger than yourself.

It doesn't matter if you've dreamed a hundred thousand dreams before, I want you to determine deep within your heart and soul that this is your time. You will not let circumstances, obstacles, dream stealers, finances, friends, sports, jobs, or anything else sidetrack you and take your focus. Commit that you will live out the rest of your days chasing your dreams and place full reliance in God that your dreams will come true in his time.

The best part about living this life is that you can live your dream starting right now. The work of your life will be done in your mind, defining and constantly clarifying your dream. The reason you aren't living your dream right now is because it is not crystal clear in your mind. Once it becomes crystallized in your mind, you will be living your dreams.

Reflections on the Riches from This Chapter

- There comes a point in all of our lives where we look back and say, "I'm glad I did" or "I wish I had."

- I will do today what other men won't so I can do tomorrow what other men can't!

- I will live like no other so I can live like no other!

- Your success is not measured by what you accumulate on earth, but by how you fulfilled the purpose for which you were created.

- Your dreams have been given to you because you are the only one who can make them come true.

- Dreams are not about what you have or don't have; it's about who you become as you move toward a dream that is bigger than yourself.

Chapter 15

FANTASY LAND

Dreams without action are nothing more than mystical fairy tales. You and I both know people who live in Fantasy Land. Fantasy Land is where dreamers who don't take action live. They are always talking about what they want and confuse that with their dream. It's always about what they are going to have and how they are going to live. They live in Fantasy Land, the land of make-believe. They have great imaginations and can wish like nothing you've ever seen, but it never goes anywhere.

I was doing a radio interview for *Born to be Rich* one time, and the radio personality asked me a question. He said that a friend of his had been talking about this dream of his for over twenty years, but he never seemed to go anywhere. The radio personality said his friend always had a great attitude and never let circumstances or obstacles dim his optimism or diminish the belief in his dream. He then asked, "So what is a person to do who believes in their dream and seems to have the right attitude but never accomplishes anything?" It's a great question because we all know people like that. So what are these people to do?

I remember a couple I worked with up in Michigan a while back. We spent hours together building their dream, defining their purpose, and creating a plan to achieve their dreams. They had a great ability to imagine the possibilities and see past where they were at that moment. They were on government assistance, but their ability to dream and keep a positive attitude was quite impressive. They also appeared to be very determined. They talked a good game and did some things that indicated they walked a good walk.

After months of working with them, I couldn't understand why they weren't farther along than they were. I was really puzzled about this, and it got me thinking about how dreams work. Why did they seem to work for some folks, and they didn't seem to do anything for others except get their hopes up, only to be exposed to everything they can't have? I finally realized what it was. They viewed dreams and success as a free ride, like government assistance. They thought one plus one equals two in the game of life and success. Sometimes one plus one hundred equals two!

It's not like a job where you work forty hours and get a paycheck. You may work four hundred hours and have just laid the groundwork, work for which you won't be paid for years to come possibly. It was never spoken, but they believed deep down that if they had this positive attitude, read an inspirational book every now and then, and spent time with me then they would become fabulously wealthy.

Needless to say, they did not become fabulously wealthy because they were not doing any work toward their plan when I wasn't around. Every excuse in the book was given at various times. One time it was because he didn't have enough work. Other times it was because there was too much work. Sometimes it was because they didn't have enough money. Other times it was because they were too tired. Success is not built on convenience! You can't wait for all the lights to be green before you pull out of the driveway. You've just got to get up and go. You have to get up and go when you don't feel like it. Does your body tell you what to do or do you tell your body what you're going to do?

I've had to drive through the night many times on my success journey so that I could put food on my table and still pursue my dream. I did what I had to do, knowing the day was coming when I would have a private jet waiting for me, and I'd be home for dinner! I'm not looking for reasons I can't do it; I'm looking for all the ways I can do both. It all comes down to action. You can have a burning desire and dream inside of you, but if you're waiting for the right time to get started, then you're setting a dangerous precedent for yourself. You have to get moving and take action. Give your dream some legs by taking action.

Your dreams will start to frustrate you if you go dream building and don't take action. You'll start asking yourself why you're looking at something you will never have. You know something your body hasn't figured out yet, and that is if you don't get busy working your plan, then you're exactly right; you will never have it. The answer to your dreams is not the lottery. It's not the sweepstakes. It is the rock-solid work ethic, dogged determination, and unwavering faith and belief that you are pursuing a much greater cause than just a tangible object.

The accomplishment of your dream is a reflection on your Creator. God doesn't make junk, and he doesn't make mistakes. He did his part; it's time you and I do ours. I'm not there yet and neither are you. We've got a lot more work that needs to be done. We have a lot more lives that need to be touched. There's a whole lot of hurting people waiting for us to enter their lives and give them a message of hope.

High school standouts can't sit at home watching the greats and become just like them. They must get out on the court and on the field and practice. They must take action. You won't become the best at what you do without taking action. It doesn't matter what kind of life you've had. It doesn't matter if you've been abused, raped, beaten, or if you have a physical handicap or impairment, you can change the course of your life by taking action toward your dreams and goals. You can use those events in your life as excuses or stepping stones. If you use them as excuses, they won. If you use them as stepping stones, you win.

Reflections on the Riches from This Chapter

- Dreams without action are nothing more than mystical fairy tales.

- Does your body tell you what to do or do you tell your body what you're going to do?

- The answer to your dreams is the rock-solid work ethic, dogged determination, and unwavering faith and belief that you are pursuing a much greater cause than just a tangible object.

Chapter 16

THAT'S NOTHING

During the fall of 2007, I took my family up into the mountains of West Virginia for the weekend. At the end of the weekend, the plan was for the girls to go up to Michigan, and I was going back to Florida. They would fly back to Florida at the end of the following week. By the time Friday night came, I was ecstatic to see them. The plan was to meet at a local restaurant. I decided to surprise them at the airport instead.

When you don't fly a lot, it makes you feel special to be greeted at the airport. I grabbed a dozen roses and made sure I had a rose for my oldest daughter as well, who was five at the time. During the week they were gone, I received the first batch of my first book, *Born to be Rich*. So with a copy of the new book in one hand and roses in the other, I stood at the edge of the security line with a host of other people waiting for their loved ones to exit the plane.

When my daughters saw me, they started running to greet me. I swooped them up as best as I could and gave them their flowers. I then told them I had a surprise. With that, I pulled the book out and showed it to them. My wife was speechless. However, without a moment's hesitation, my five-year-old daughter said, "Well, that's nothing. I got a new princess keychain!" And she pulled it slowly from her pocket.

I was stunned. In an instant, she equated a new keychain on the same magnitude as the nationwide release of a book her father wrote! She immediately grounded me that day. I started to laugh as I said, "You're right, that is nothing! Let me see your new keychain!" She reminded me that taking what's most important to my family and making it the most important thing to me is what makes dreams come true.

We naturally tend to live in past successes. We talk about the deals we used to do and the trades we used to make. I thought about the success I've had in stocks, real estate, careers, and various businesses I've owned and said to myself, "That's nothing!"

You may have just gone through or are going through some hard times. You may be facing extraordinary amounts of rejection or experiencing one of the lowest points of your life right now, but you need to say to yourself, "That's nothing." In contrast, you may have just closed the biggest deal of your life. You may have just set a new record or achieved a major accomplishment, and you need to celebrate, then say, "That's nothing." As a side note, I should mention that this should only be said to yourself to motivate you to move on and not live in the past. It should never be said to someone sharing their dreams or accomplishments with you!

Are you looking at success as the finish line or the starting line? Realize it's just the beginning and not the end. Celebrate your victories along the way. There are many successful people that simply don't realize how great they can become if they'd only learn to say, "That's nothing!" You aren't in competition with anyone but yourself. You don't have to beat their record; you just have to beat yours. You don't have to take from anybody to get ahead; you just have to exceed your past performance. The person who owns the house you want isn't your competitor. The person who drives the car you want isn't your enemy. You don't have to compete—create!

I know it can be frustrating. Things don't always turn out the way we thought they would. People you thought would buy your product or service might not. Those closest to you said they would meet you at a certain place at a certain time, and they didn't. People told you they would do this and do that, and they never did. You thought you'd achieve a higher level of success by this point in your life than you have. You may be discouraged with your life right now. You may be discouraged with your dreams and goals at this moment. You may be discouraged with things that should have worked out and they never did. I want you to say, "That's nothing!" and keep moving forward. When you fail, tell yourself, "That's nothing." When you succeed, tell yourself, "That's nothing." When you're rejected, say, "That's nothing." When you have accomplished everything you possibly can, say, "That's nothing." You aren't too young to realize your dreams and be successful. You aren't too old to realize your dreams and be successful.

It's not how hard you fall, but how high you bounce the counts. You are a winner, regardless of what the circumstances around you might say. You are destined for greatness. It is your responsibility—no, it is your duty—to look the circumstances that are getting you discouraged and keeping you down in the eye and say, "That's nothing!" Here are five attributes of a dreamer.

1. Dreamers are passionate about what they do.

   Pay the price without counting the cost. Give everything you do everything you have. Passion will create favor in your life.

2. Dreamers have a sense of urgency with a spirit of expectancy.

Don't procrastinate. Don't put off until tomorrow what you can do today. Make the next phone call. Call the next prospect. Follow up with the potential lead. Expect them to do what you ask them to do. Keep your word. Be on time to appointments. Don't make people wait on you. I don't ever want to be called "The late Rollan Roberts" as long as I'm alive!

3. Dreamers don't quit when tough times come.

Robert Schuller titled a book *Tough Times Never Last, but Tough People Do.* No one is exempt from difficult times and seemingly insurmountable opposition. The difference always comes down to giving it one more shot. It's going for it one more time. It's getting back up once you get knocked down.

4. Dreamers believe they have what it takes to achieve their dreams.

Dreamers believe in themselves. They believe the accomplishment of their dream is merely a matter of time, persistence, and focus on their part. Dreamers believe that success lies within themselves and not in the circumstances of life.

5. Dreamers control their thoughts.

You are, or soon will be, what you think about. Dreamers control what they think and do not let their thoughts be a result of whatever conversations are going on around them. They exercise mental focus and discipline. I can tell you the name of the person who told me not to start a business because it was too risky. I can tell you the name of the person who told me I couldn't build a successful business. I can tell you the name of the person who told me not to pursue my education. But dreamers control what they think. I heard them, but I did not listen to them. I just said to myself, "That's nothing!"

Reflections on the Riches from This Chapter

☞ Taking what's most important to your family and making it the most important thing to you is what makes dreams come true.

☞ There are many successful people who simply don't realize how great they can become if they'd only learn to say, "That's nothing!"

☞ It is your responsibility—no, it is your duty—to look the circumstances that are getting you discouraged and keeping you down in the eye and say, "That's nothing!"

☞ Dreamers believe that success lies within themselves and not in the circumstances of life.

Chapter 17

WINGING IT

Many people today have an idea of the life they want to live. They can spout off some semblance of a dream if asked. But when you start asking for specifics, it becomes blatantly obvious that they don't have much of a plan at all. They are simply winging it, playing life by ear.

A friend of mine, multi-millionaire businessman Jeff Levitan, fell into this category as a young man. At nineteen he lacked goals, dreams, self-discipline, and mentorship. He was simply drifting through life and winging it. Jeff grew up in a lower-middle-class home where his father was a truck driver and his mother was a waitress. Money was sparse and tight, and  like the majority of homes where money is sparse and tight, it caused much strain and stress on the household. The parental relationship was strained due to the lack of finances. Jeff was only eight years old at the time, but he determined at that point that he never wanted to be without money. It wasn't that he dreamed of big houses and a lot of material things; he dreamed of a peaceful, happy home where money wasn't an issue.

Jeff hit one of the lowest points of his life during college. Living in a rented basement bedroom, his life hit the financial skids. As he faced potential ruin and the house of cards came crashing around him, he determined to pick himself up by the boot straps, get his eyes off of his circumstances, and get focused on solutions and goals. It was during this time Jeff learned that successful people don't avoid risk, they manage it. Jeff said, "Most people think the opposite of security is risk. Truth is, the opposite of security is opportunity."

After graduating from college, Jeff took a job at an insurance company. He quickly realized that the corporate life was not for him. He did not like the lack of flexibility and creativity that came with antiquated processes and policies. Shortly thereafter, he started his business. At thirty years of age and within five years of the launch, he had gone from a negative net worth (and self-worth) to millionaire. Five years from that point, he was making over $1,000,000 per year!

This kind of success doesn't just happen without focus and energy. Jeff kept his full-time day job and worked his business full time outside of regular business hours. For eight solid months, he went to work during the day at the insurance company and left each evening to work on his business, which he did until around midnight, day in and day out. He didn't grab the golf clubs, tennis racquet, or fishing pole on the weekends either. He invested his entire weekend for eight straight months fighting for his freedom. Jeff chose to buy his freedom in eight months by working hard as an entrepreneur instead of through forty or fifty years as an employee. Jeff likes to say, "The tougher you are on yourself, the easier life is on you; the easier you are on yourself, the harder life is on you."

That doesn't mean that you never fall on hard times. There were distinct moments in time when Jeff wanted to hang it all up and just quit. A few months after he started his business, he wasn't seeing the kind of results (cash in hand) that he expected. His vision was collapsing, and his dream was deflating quickly. What got Jeff through this difficult time was the wisdom of his mentor. He realized that he was making decisions based on his past experiences. Because he was going to a financial place he had never been, he did not know what the journey looked like, so he wasn't qualified to say whether he was succeeding or not, but his mentor was. Jeff compares this time in each of our lives as the germination process. It's the time when rapid growth is happening, but it's happening under the soil and surface, so it's harder to recognize, but you know it is there.

We aren't tempted to quit just when things are tough. You will be tempted to quit when things are going great as well. That's why you need a dream that's tied to your purpose and not just a reward. After Jeff had achieved great success, he semi-retired and moved to South Florida as a young man. He heard so many people tell him that he should be on a boat somewhere living it up that he agreed with them and did. Unfortunately, he let others less successful than himself influence him negatively. Sixty days later, he was bored. Ninety days later, he opened another office and got back in the business of making a difference in other people's lives. He realized his life had a greater meaning and purpose than merely a lavish existence.

One of the most important lessons that Jeff has taught me is that I can handle much more than I think I can. "Maximize your capacity," is what he would say. "What's possible for you?" he would ask. Stop focusing on the past. Jeff has said,

"Try driving down the road at seventy miles per hour looking in the rearview mirror and see what happens." But that's how many of us live our lives. To live your dreams and enjoy the journey, you have to learn from the past, not get stuck in it. Focus on where you are going.

Today, Jeff is extremely blessed and uses those blessings to bless and enrich the lives of those less fortunate. Jeff started a foundation that is currently building orphanages and schools in Africa, Central America, and the Philippines. He serves as the senior vice chairman and is an executive board member for the company he is a part of. He has seventy-five offices (and counting) across twenty-four states (and counting) with four thousand associates (and counting). He was selected as the Naperville, Illinois Entrepreneur of the Year in 2005. If Jeff could talk to you right now, he would say that you deserve to win. You deserve to have all of your dreams come true and live a fulfilled life. Don't just wing your life; maximize your capacity and live your life on purpose!

Reflections on the Riches from This Chapter

- Most people think the opposite of security is risk. Truth is, the opposite of security is opportunity.

- Choose to buy your freedom by working hard as an entrepreneur instead of through forty or fifty years as an employee.

- The tougher you are on yourself, the easier life is on you; the easier you are on yourself, the harder life is on you.

- You need a dream that's tied to your purpose and not just a reward.

- Don't just wing your life; maximize your capacity and live your life on purpose!

Chapter 18

WHEN THE END ISN'T
THE END

I t happens all the time. People accomplish their dream, and they retire. They're done, finished. They have no more great accomplishments or achievements. It's easy to forget that the excitement and power of a dream is in the pursuit of the dream, not just in the attainment of the dream.

It is certainly a worthy goal to retire early. Historically, however, retirement is a relatively new concept. Retirement was created with the Industrial Age. After working a regular job for forty years, people would retire, get a gold watch, and die in two years. With the advent of the social security system, a standard retirement age was established.

Thinking like a business owner and investor, there is no such thing as retirement. Most people don't stop doing what they love. That's why Bobby Bowden, the Florida State University football coach, is still coaching at seventy-nine years of age. It also explains Joe Paterno, head coach at Penn State, who is eighty-one and still coaching college football and going strong. Retirement isn't an age; it's being free to do what you want to do with your life! You can do that at twenty-five or you can do it at sixty-five; it's your choice.

One of my friends and mentors, Sandy Sansing, taught me that the end doesn't have to, and probably shouldn't, be the end. Sandy came from a middle-class family and was taught at an early age the value of hard work and a strong work ethic. He and his dad used to sit up at night and talk about successful people and what it took to be successful. Some of the best advice Sandy  ever received from his dad was, "Son, do your best. If you make an A or an F, just do your best."

He excelled in school and throughout college. When he wasn't playing college golf, Sandy was bagging groceries and working construction jobs. After graduating from college with an accounting degree, he took a job as a salesman with one of the three major computer firms at that time. After a three-week sales course, he hit the pavement with hardware under his arm. Armed with a strong work ethic and total persistence, he began to succeed with the company. In fact, he ended up becoming the youngest sales manager in the company's history.

Sandy knew he didn't want to work for someone else his entire life and had a dream to own a business. Notice his dream was not to become a multimillionaire, but to own a business that could put food on the table. He valued his freedom and was passionate about entrepreneurship. With this in mind, he decided to go to law school. He went in to work and resigned. However, his boss would not accept his resignation and talked him into staying. That's not the first time a company has stolen someone's dream. He kept plugging away at the daily grind.

Finally, the frustration of working for someone else became too overwhelming to ignore. He and another employee at the company decided to start a business. They both went in to resign on the same day. Once again, the boss tried to talk him into staying. This time, he threatened to sue him if he resigned and started a competing business. But Sandy was determined and resigned from the industry-leading company.

That was one of the most fearful times of his life. The night before he resigned, he talked it over with his dad. He asked his dad if he was making a mistake. It seemed like such a risky move. His dad said, "This is your dream. I'd hate to see you look back and think 'What if?' You can always go get another job if it doesn't work out." Sandy agreed. Risk is only risk if you have something to lose. He had nothing to lose, but he did risk years and sanity since he was only twenty-seven when he resigned to start the business. As Sandy says, "When you start with no money, your goal is survival!"

He and his partner did start the business and sure enough, his previous employer sued for breach of their noncompete agreements. This action forced them to start selling out of state. They went to a bank and applied for a business loan. The banker asked Sandy where his offices were located. He said that they were still in the selection process of a few of the high-end commercial offices. The banker asked him who is lawyer was, and he said they were still interviewing lawyers. The banker asked who his accountant was, and he said they were still reviewing the major accounting firms to see who was most competent to handle their business. The banker asked for a business card, and he said they were being printed. The banker looked at him and said, "You don't have a thing, do you?" He replied, "No, ma'am, I don't have a thing." Sandy earned the banker's trust that day and ended up getting a loan to get the business launched. He didn't take a paycheck for the first nine months of the business. There were many times throughout that first year that he wanted to quit. He even interviewed in case he needed to get a job quickly. He started taking $150 per week from the business after nine months in business, but that only lasted five weeks because the business couldn't afford it. At the end of the first year, they were out of money and had an unhappy client base. They were a struggling little company trying to fight corporate giants such as IBM.

If the business was going to survive, they needed to get to Atlanta to exhibit their product at a big convention. Since he did not have enough money to go to the convention, and the convention was his only hope of survival, he had to get another loan. Sandy went to another bank and was able to get a loan. Off to Atlanta they went! He was so excited. They were so passionate about their product. Just before the convention ended, Sandy called a couple of his competitors over and demonstrated his product for them. He expected them to be in awe of what their product could do. What he didn't know was that he was just about to enter into the lowest point of his life. After his competitors saw the product that he was absolutely in love with and had spent the last year paying a high price with little results, they said, "Get a new business; you'll never make it."

Sandy and his partner packed up their display and started making the drive home. It was the longest—and quietest—ride of his life. They just sat in silence. They had given their all to the business. They had given their heart, soul, passion, sweat, finances, talents, and time to growing this business that not only was dying, but was apparently doomed for utter failure. Once they arrived home, they just sat there deciding what to do next. Do we abandon the business, get a job, and get on with life? Do we quit? During the next few minutes, they decided to quit trying to be all things to all people. They chose one market and determined to dominate it. Sandy hit the road the next six weeks going to industry-specific conventions within their target vertical. They eventually began adding additional salespeople to the organization. In order to pay them, Sandy went from having to sell two units a month to one unit a week! Sandy did what he had to do and executed when it counted the most. He went on trips that he couldn't come home from until he had the check.

The company began to take hold and get off the ground. Four and a half years from the day they launched, they sold the business, and Sandy became a multimillionaire at thirty-two years old! Most people would have retired. They would have joined the country club and spent their lives traveling, boating, and golfing. But what could have been the end wasn't the end.

By this time, Sandy had two young children. He began to think about his legacy and the example he would set for his kids. His dad instilled such a strong work ethic in him, and he wanted to raise his kids the same way. He ended up taking much of the money he had made and investing it in a Chevrolet dealership. Within a year, the once-profitable car dealership began losing money. He started having problems with sales and employees. Things started turning around the next year. Two years later, he bought a Nissan dealership. Five years later, he was offered the opportunity to be a BMW dealer.

Today, Sandy owns six successful car dealerships, including Chevrolet, Nissan, BMW, Mazda, Chrysler, and Mini Coopers. He is a national board member of the Fellowship of Christian Athletes and sits or has sat on the board of directors of banks, hospitals, education institutions, and an orphanage. His BMW dealership has been ranked number one in customer satisfaction for many years. He has been awarded the Center of Excellence, Dealers of Excellence, and President's Club awards from BMW, the Circle of Excellence and President's Club award from Nissan, and the Mark of Excellence award from Chevrolet many times over. Sandy's success story is not over. In fact, it's still being written because what could be the end isn't the end!

Reflections on the Riches from This Chapter

- The excitement and power of a dream is in the pursuit of the dream, not just in the attainment of the dream.

- Retirement isn't an age; it's being free to do what you want to do with your life!

- Risk is only risk if you have something to lose.

Chapter 19

WHEN THE DREAM DRIES UP

ThHere is a major difference between winners who win and champions who win. What makes a Michael Jordan come out of retirement? Is winning title after title not enough? Why does Tiger Woods keep playing the same championships year after year after he's won them all? Why do superstars in many of the sports come out of retirement? Why do many of these athletes push themselves when their reputation and legend don't demand it? Don't they risk losing the credibility they spent years establishing? Should champions "go out on top?" What makes champions want to take another stab at victory?

There are a lot of winners at every level of sports. There are few champions. One of those champions is Shannon Miller. She is the most decorated American gymnast, male or female, of all time. She has earned seven Olympic medals and nine World Championship medals since 1990. She won five medals at the 1992 Olympics, which were the

most medals won by a United States athlete. In her career, she has won fifty-eight international and forty-nine national competition medals—over half of which have been gold. She won two gold medals at the 1996 Olympics and is now a member of five halls of fame, including the United States Olympic Hall of Fame and the International Gymnastics Hall of Fame. The answers to the questions above can be found in Shannon's story.

Like all champions, her life has not been lived from Olympic gold medal to Olympic gold medal. There were valleys. There were hard times. There were unexpected circumstances. There were challenges and obstacles that appeared insurmountable at the worst possible times. Shannon was born with her legs growing inward, not exactly the best hand to be dealt if you want to become a world-class gymnast! She wore a brace for six months to correct the condition. When she was eight, the small gym she belonged to raised money for a few of them to go to Russia for a two-week camp. That was the turning point from recreational to competitive gymnastics. She did not make some unwavering, steadfast commitment at a young age to focus on gymnastics and go to the Olympics. She did it because she enjoyed it, loved it, and had fun doing it. It also provided a great outlet for her since she was naturally shy.

There was one notable time in her career when she wanted to quit. She was coming home from the gym crying every day and did not know why. She told her parents and coaches that she wanted to quit. Over the next few weeks, her coaches did some smart things to help Shannon find her passion and love for the sport again. Ultimately, the passion and love had to come from within. The truth she discovered about herself during this time is a golden gem: you have to have a goal! What do you set as a goal when you've won medals at the Olympics, won gold medals at the World Championships, and won every other major event? In retrospect, she realized that she wanted to quit because she wasn't aiming for anything specific and was at a loss for goals. She didn't have a big enough dream or goal to pay the price required of an elite athlete. Once she identified the problem, she was able to look for something worthwhile to shoot for that was worth all of the hard work and discipline.

At the beginning of each calendar year, her coach made the team write down their short and long term goals. Many of the girls would write down "Go to the Olympics" or "Win a gold medal." Shannon saw things a little differently. Those dreams were too big for where she was in gymnastics at that time. While that may have been the appropriate answer—and certainly the standard answer for most of them—she would always list skills and techniques that she wanted to perfect in the short and long term.

The goals you set to accomplish your dreams should be in sight and out of reach. They have to be close enough to home that you can wrap your arms around them and believe them. It's hard to hug a cloud! Shannon never walked into a competition saying, "This one's mine; I'm winning the gold." Instead, her attitude was always, "I'm going to do my best. I'm not going to do the minimum level of difficulty to win. I'm going to push myself to be my best and perform with excellence." This mentality allowed her to shine at the right moment, in the right place, and in the right time. Every day doesn't have to be victorious, but you have to execute in crunch time. Each day is either a building day, battling day, or banner day. Most days are building days. Every day can't be a banner day, and not all days will be battling days. Understanding this cycle will help you execute at the right place at the right time.

Shannon is known for taking great risks in competition

that she may not have had to take to win. I asked Shannon about this because I've taken risks that people felt I didn't need to take. What they didn't understand was that it wasn't a risk to me. It was what I had to do to see what I was capable of. The risk is not so much in losing money; the risk lies in not knowing what might have been. Shannon wanted to be excellent. If her goal was just to win, she would have done the easier skills. Shannon said, "You don't play it safe just to win." The more you win, the more you are expected to win. The pressure others place on you to succeed increases with each success.

She also pointed out that she decided early on to master the skills that all the other girls feared. Whatever they were scared of, she wanted to excel at. The beam is the scariest apparatus for most female gymnasts, so Shannon determined to master it. So while many of the other girls were practicing what they enjoyed, Shannon found pleasure in doing what others feared. That is one of the master keys to becoming great and fulfilling your dreams. You have to delight in the process and the work of becoming great. The obsession is not so much in winning the gold medals in life, but it is in mastering the disciplines, skills, and techniques that you have chosen to pursue. It is about becoming the absolute best at what you do by finding pleasure in the work. This philosophy paid off for Shannon as she became known as the "Beam Queen."

I'll never forget how Shannon handled one devastating unexpected circumstance. Four months before the 1992 Olympics, she dislocated and broke her elbow on the last dismount of the practice. The team doctor told her they were going to put her arm in a sling, and she was done for three months. Her first Olympic dream started disappearing fast. The doctor provided an alternative that would require her to pay a huge price with consequences she would live with forever. They could have emergency surgery that day and reattach the bone with a screw in her elbow and be out for two weeks instead of waiting for it to heal naturally over three months. She immediately made the decision to undergo surgery. She spent the following day getting over the anesthesia and went back to the gym the next day. She spent the next two weeks sitting in splits watching the rest of her team train. Most people would have walked around the gym, socialized, and hung out. Not Shannon. She sat in the splits for hours at a time to stay as limber as possible.

Some winners take shortcuts, but champions do not. That is a mark of greatness. No one would have blamed her if she just sat around the gym watching everyone train. The heart of a champion would not let her do that. You can get by with working less, but that's not the action a dreamer takes. If your goal is to lose weight, it's not okay to eat diet food in front of people and gorge privately. If you are passionate about what you are doing, you will do what you can when you can. You will look for reasons why you should, not for reasons why you should not. The sweetness of victory comes from the remembrance of all the challenges and obstacles you overcame to get to where you are.

One of the most powerful lessons I've learned from Shannon is the power of having no regrets. Shannon won silver at the 1992 Olympics, won gold at the 1996 Olympics, and had dominated the sport of gymnastics for years. She toured for a while following the 1996 Olympics and then stopped training for competition. Eight months before the 2000 Olympics, she started thinking about going for another Olympics. She hadn't been training for two years! She started asking herself if she still had it in her to compete at that level. She had a loss of goals at the time, so she decided to go for it. She felt she had more inside her to give and wanted to get back in the hunt.

Most people would not have made that choice. She risked embarrassment. She risked not making the team. She risked the hit her pride would take by not being the best in the world or being beaten by a younger gymnast. Shannon made the choice to go for it because the real risk lay in knowing that she'd have to live the rest of her life wondering what might have been. The "what if" drove her to keep going. She did not make the team that year, but she did not fail. Failure would have been in not trying. You will live the rest of your life saying, "I'm glad I did" or "I wish I had." Which one will you be saying about the choices you're making?

Reflections on the Riches from This Chapter

☞ The goals you set to accomplish your dreams should be in sight and out of reach.

☞ Each day is either a building day, battling day, or banner day. Most days are building days.

☞ Don't play it safe just to win.

☞ Delight in the process and the work of becoming great.

☞ The obsession is not so much in winning the gold medals in life, but it is in mastering the disciplines, skills, and techniques that you have chosen to pursue.

☞ Failure is not in losing; it is in not trying.

Chapter 20

POWER OF PERSONAL AFFIRMATIONS

Personal affirmations have helped me tremendously. I heard an affirmation one time that is many a dreamer's sentiment. It went like this:

> We the willing led by the unknowing are doing the impossible for the ungrateful. We have done so much for so long with so little that we are now qualified to do anything with nothing.

It is so easy to quit in this day and age. It has become acceptable for people to quit anything they don't want to do anymore. One of the reasons many people don't win is because they quit and jumped into something else before they gained enough traction to be successful. And they get so impatient for success in what they jumped into that they eventually quit that for the next carrot. Their life is cyclical in nature.

Persistence and consistency are the primary things I knew I could be good at. Regardless of my talent as compared to others, I knew I could outlast the competition. I found that you can win by default because you're the last person standing. It doesn't mean you're necessarily the best, but you did last! Make consistency and perseverance your niche.

You may not be good at very many things. You may not have a single trait for which you are known. You may not have extraordinary musical, sports, or business acumen, but anybody can keep going. Quitting is not an option. When you come to a roadblock, persist. When you come face to face with failure, persist. When every bone in your body wants to quit and walk away, persist!

I'll never forget hearing the story of the gold prospector in California who invested all of his earnings into purchasing a property that he believed had gold. He dug for years and poured everything he had (money, sweat, time, etc.) into mining for gold. Broke and discouraged, he threw in the towel and sold the land to a farmer who was going to let his animals graze on it. Shortly thereafter, the farmer was using a post-hole digger to install a fence when he struck one of the largest gold reserves in California. The gold prospector had dug in that area many times before, but he quit digging just a few feet from gold! Don't stop digging; your success breakthrough is just around the corner. It's in the next shovel full of dirt. Persist!

I still have several affirmations that I repeat depending on the circumstance or the thought. I have a specific affirmation I repeat the moment a thought about financial lack enters my mind. The second I start to think "I can't afford it," I start repeating the affirmation until I forgot what started it. I want to chase thoughts of poverty and lack far from me. Affirmations helped raise my level of belief that I could accomplish great things with my life. It was the repetitious nature of my daily affirmations that instilled a confidence in me that it was okay to shoot for the moon, make money, reach for my dreams, and actually try to become everything I had imagined becoming.

I am often asked what my affirmation is. I don't have a magical chant or some mystical saying that I hum, but I do have a creed that I say out loud each day and live by. I call it "The Dreamer's Creed." I invite every dreamer to say the Dreamer's Creed out loud every day. Even though I wrote this as my personal affirmation, I give it to you. It is for all of those dreamers who are shooting for the moon and refuse to quit. It's for those of you who have determined that this is your life's purpose, mission, and dream, and no sacrifice is too great in the realization of your dream. You can't read this and quit chasing your dreams even if the times are hard. If you are willing to give your dream every fiber of your being from now until you are taken from this life, this creed is for you. Say it with me.

The Dreamer's Creed

I am fearfully and wonderfully made as a creative being in the image of God and have been equipped with the power, belief, and strength to succeed in living a happy, healthy, wealthy lifestyle full of life, vitality, and energy. I am hardworking, discerning, diligent, prudent, focused, challenged, motivated, and patient and am a good steward of my time, money, and energy. I am a blessed and highly favored winner that attracts unlimited riches, wealth, and prosperity into my life so that I may give freely to others and worthy causes. I will honor God with my success, for God's wisdom is the key to my success. This is my day. Today is the day God will give me a financial breakthrough. Today's miracle will change my life forever and set me on a course to riches and wealth. I will not give up, let up, or shut up until I'm taken up. My dream is a direct fulfillment of my purpose, and I cannot and will not shirk or relinquish my God-given duty to pursue my God-given dream every day with every ounce of energy I have.

My Story

I was born in Birmingham, Alabama. Our family moved to Florida when I was five years old. We lived there for four years while my dad went to college. He graduated with a Biblical Studies major and became a pastor in West Virginia as well as the Administrator of their Christian academy. My mother has her bachelor's degree in Secondary Education and has taught in that school from that day until now. Upon my high school graduation, I moved to Knoxville, Tennessee to go to college. I got my Bachelor's degree in five semesters. It was a major accomplishment for me. However, that is not the only thing I achieved during this short time frame. My parents were not able to provide much financial support for my college bills, and I did not want to get student loans. I worked a full time job during my college years from 3pm until midnight Monday through Friday. On Saturday and Sunday, I worked as an intern an hour and a half away from the college. At 20 years old, I walked across that stage and received my college diploma with a net worth of $700,000. My goal was to be worth one million dollars. I fell short, but I was not too disappointed with all of my accomplishments. I would reach one million in net worth within four months of graduation. I got cocky and content with what I had. I bought a bunch of things. I started letting my past successes keep me from taking care of business. My lack of focus and attention proved disastrous. This circumstance jolted me back to reality and jerked me down off of my high horse. I was back into the reality that my past decision making had created for me.

Those were some of the darkest days that I would go through. I remember my Dad saying, "Well, you were worth more than most people will ever be worth, and you are poorer than most people will ever be." He was right. I had been on both extremes, and I was going through the worst financial nightmare anyone can imagine. I remember trying to find 15-20 cents to go to the grocery store to buy ramen noodles only to realize that I didn't have enough gas in the car to make it to the grocery store a mile away. I remember putting 30 cents into the gas tank to go to the grocery store and buying 25 cents worth of groceries. It was the most humbling time of my life. It's hard for an empty bag to stand up straight, and I had the wind knocked out of me. I remember sitting out by the lake and thinking to myself, "This is the poorest I will ever be the rest of my life." I determined in those dark days that I would never again lose sight of my business. I would never rest on my laurels and think that I had arrived. I committed to myself that I was a winner and that whatever it took, I would rebuild my financial empire, and I would be richer than I ever had hoped to be.

I moved from the lake house to a 900 square foot apartment. Nine months later, I moved into a home that was worth more than twice the amount of our lake house. I had paid off all of our debt. We were back on track. Nothing was going to keep us down! Everyone gets knocked down, but it takes a winner to get back up and keep going.

I've had money, and I've been broke – and rich is certainly better! I love it when I hear that a true millionaire could do it all over again and probably quicker because of his financial education and the lessons that he learned. I have learned what not to do. I know how to get wealthy when you have money and when you have less than nothing. No matter what your current financial situation, you can be rich. You might have to be more creative the more difficult your situation, but it is possible. The worse things got, the more creative I had to be. That creativity has served me well. Thank you for allowing me to inspire you to pursue your dreams!

Rollan A. Roberts II

The Dream Builder

rollan@idream247.com
www.rollanroberts.com
www.idream247.com